D1238881

Pierre Rival
Photographs Christian Sarramon

Gourmet Bistros and Restaurants of Paris

The city's finest tables

Flammarion

Contents

8

Paris, Restaurant Capital of the World

Paris invented the restaurant at the end of the eighteenth century. Since then, the City of Light has remained the world capital of restaurants, and of gastronomic excellence in general. This is where the bistro and the brasserie originated, and it was the birthplace of the "concept" restaurant and the "decor" restaurant. Some of the most innovative and unusual approaches to the art of dining, later propagated all over the world, first saw the light of day here. Paris takes its restaurants seriously: they are as much a part of its culture as its most famous monuments.

14

Historic Settings

Interiors that would not be out of place in a museum, food that is of the very highest caliber, and locations to die for, all in existence for at least the last century. These establishments are never a disappointment for those who see the restaurant experience as a nostalgic journey back in time. A gallery of famous names, including Le Grand Véfour, Les Ambassadeurs, Lapérouse, Le Procope, Alain Ducasse, Le Meurice, and Maxim's.

56

Brasseries

Brasseries are as much a part of Paris as the café tables spilling out onto terraces and the booksellers on the banks of the Seine. They welcome travelers leaving train stations and many have been a refuge for artists and writers. Today they continue to play a central role in the social life of the capital, where all strata mix and meet in a celebration of appetizing, no-nonsense food.

Page 2: Le Square Trousseau, not far from the Bastille, still true to its nineteenth-century origins as a working-man's bistro.
Preceding page: The cozily designed interior and relaxed attitude to food at Philippe Starck's restaurant Bon are representative of the new trends in luxury dining in Paris.

84
Bistros

The number of bistros in Paris has grown considerably over the last ten years. They have been fostering a culinary revolution, reinventing classic French dishes with a more rustic approach. Allard, Aux Lyonnais, and L'Ami Louis are some of the places where Parisians go to find the tastes and aromas of home cooking.

114
Contemporary Settings

The great interior designers of today—Jacques Garcia, Terence Conran, Olivier Gagnère, Pierre-Yves Rochon, and Philippe Starck—have created the settings for the food of the future. Their designs are vastly diverse: L'Ambroisie, Le Bélier, L'Alcazar, Cristal Room, Pinxo, L'Atelier de Joël Robuchon, Le Chiberta, Le Café Marly, and Georges.

161
Gourmet Guidebook

The addresses of all the legendary restaurants featured, and a large selection of other interesting places to eat.

To Cherche-Midi

Paris's restaurants are institutions.

The city may no longer be the center of the international art market, the French language may have ceased to be the language of diplomacy and cultured nobility the world over, and literature and theater may thrive elsewhere, but when it comes to food and restaurants, Paris is still the place that matters. The style of cooking that is internationally regarded as "classic" is essentially French: cooking schools from around the world have borrowed techniques and presentation styles from French cuisine for at least three hundred years. This privileged position is not to be attributed to some genius for creativity on the part of the French, nor even to the diversity of France's regional produce. Other countries rightly pride themselves on having similarly rich culinary resources, and there are other cultures with over a thousand years' experience in the art of transforming simple foodstuffs into morsels of delight. The abiding status of Paris as world capital of restaurants must be due, above all, to the special importance the French place on culinary passion. Gastronomy is no minor art, not simply a service intended to satisfy an inevitable need; it is a real artifact of civilization, a constituent part of the French identity as important as the language or the shared references to a common past.

This attitude can be seen in the position Parisian chefs hold in the cultural life of the city. They are considered true artists, whose recipes and techniques are discussed in learned tones by devotees, whether or not they have been to their restaurants. To a foreigner, it can seem paradoxical that gastronomy should be the subject of so much talking: in Paris it is certainly a subject of debate that is taken just as seriously as politics or sports. The reason for this resides partly in the fact that two styles of cooking, *cuisine savante,* which has graced the highest tables since before the Revolution, and the more popularly influenced *cuisine bourgeoise* one finds in a bistro, have never lost sight of each other. The refinements of the former tend to find their way to the domestic stoves, while with the latter, a regard for consistency and a respect for produce have held professionals back from baroque temptations. There is a dense network of catering schools in France, led by the famous École Ferrandi in Paris, which continuously transmit their extensive body of knowledge. Expertise is also passed on through the hierarchy of kitchen staff in grand hotels and luxury restaurants, and shared within the kitchens of family-owned establishments. For Parisians, the tradition of punctuating one's social life at fixed times during the day has also sharpened the desire to eat well, and to treat the occasion as an opportunity for everybody to meet and relax. That is why Paris decorates

its restaurants as it used to its cathedrals. The Revolution has passed, the cathedrals have been emptied of their treasures, and the restaurants have bloomed in their place, designed by the best architects, decorated by the best artists, and ornamented by the best craftsmen.

This book is a promenade through the best restaurants in Paris, which also means the most beautiful ones, since great cooking thrives in a purpose-made setting, and nowhere are the settings finer than in Paris. As we shall see, since the eighteenth century, the best restaurants have prided themselves on their decor, whether harking back to a previous age or aiming squarely for the taste of the day. Some magnificent examples of Art Nouveau and Art Deco have survived in the restaurants of Paris. More recently, a new wave of establishments has turned to contemporary design and even a "post-historic" style that mixes references to the old with the conceptual boldness of the avant-garde—a very Parisian idea of harmony. Architects and designers like Jacques Garcia, Patrick Jouin, Philippe Starck, and Jean-Michel Wilmotte started off by decorating restaurants in Paris before working all over the world. From the dining rooms of the top hotels to corner bistros, the trend is now toward not only more spectacular decoration, but also the pursuit of a new level of conviviality around a table. There are now in-store restaurants, and restaurants where kitchens open directly onto the eating area. French table service, which was once considered overly formal, is lightening up without losing any of its quality. In Paris you can enjoy all the ceremony of your waiter carving at your table, or thrill in anticipation as you enjoy the spectacle of your meal being prepared at a counter-top kitchen. From every way you look at it, a trip to the gourmet Paris of today offers a complete experience. From one restaurant to the next, you can be plunged into history then immersed in a vision of the future. You can wander off the street into the nineteenth century or be catapulted into a kaleidoscopic vision of the bustle of the twenty-first. You can choose whether to savor the eternal dishes of classic French cooking, or give in to the giddiness of cutting-edge culinary creation. Paris has all it needs to appeal to both the nostalgic and the adventurous. And that, as always, is the source of its charm.

*Page 8: Le Café Marly facing the pyramid at the Louvre, two examples
where the modern has successfully been integrated into the ancient.
Preceding pages: Turn-of-the-century representation of the Nice carnival on
the ceiling of Le Train Bleu, the station buffet that looks more like a palace.
Facing page: an unusual view of the seafood station at Terence Conran's L'Alcazar,
near Saint-Germain-des-Prés, before the oysters and shellfish are delivered.*

Historic Settings

Museums of Gastronomy

PRUNIER

*Detail of the bar at Prunier
with its Art Deco mosaics
(preceding page).*

LE PROCOPE

*With no great concern
for anachronism, Le Procope
juxtaposes the libertine
eighteenth century
and the romantic nineteenth
(facing page).*

A historical account of the finest restaurants in Paris could start with the story of one of the most resounding flops in the history of catering. The hero of this disaster is one Belloni, a great actor turned café-owner at the beginning of the eighteenth century, much admired by Parisians for his portrayal of Pierrot (Watteau's famous painting of a Pierrot in the Louvre, known as *Gilles*, may actually have been used as a sign for the café). Belloni decided to capitalize on his reputation and open an establishment to serve food to the public. A contemporary account by the Parfaict brothers, chroniclers of the French theater, contains this anecdote:

> Belloni being applauded by all publics, wanted still to enhance his reputation by joining with the ranks of Victualers. To this end, and having paid for such privileges as were necessary, he set up a shoppe on the rue de Petits-Champs, opposite the small passage leading to the Saint-Honoré cloister. The ceiling above the door bore the likenesses of divers Italian Actors, including his own, with the inscription "Au Caffé Comique." This title, along with Belloni's name, brought great popularity to the place, but its glory was destroyed in a moment by a candle end. One morning when many patrons were gathered there, one chanced to spy in his cup, in which some Coffee had just been poured for him, some thing, which he examined with care and recognized it to be a candle end. We shall curtail our account of the remainder of the scene, which was most mortifying for the Victualer-Actor. All shewed their disgust, and all unanimously promised him never more to set foot in his Caffé. He was talked to by nobody; and that very day, his shoppe was as deserted as it had been full theretofore.

This was in 1710 or 1712, at a time when coffee had become a fashionable drink, and Belloni should have been able to make a success of his venture. But by staking everything on his popularity as an actor, he forgot the quintessential importance of both setting and service. His establishment became indistinguishable from the "places of congregation and refuge for thieves, swindlers and other wrongdoers

LE PROCOPE

*A hotbed for subversion?
Under Chopin's gaze, the
weapons of the Revolution
on the wallpaper remind us of
the role the restaurant played as
a club for the sans-culottes
(above and facing page).*

and dissolute types" denounced in a contemporary police ruling. In other words, Belloni's Caffé Comique was no more than a smoky, ill-lit tavern where all manner of shady dealings were likely to take place.

What a contrast with Le Procope, which was opened in 1689 (although some sources say 1702) by an Italian from Palermo. Francesco Procopio dei Coltelli started at the bottom of the catering ladder—as so many restaurateurs would from then on—serving coffee at the Saint-Germain fair. Procopio's strong business sense led him to respect principles that, for the great Parisian food establishments that followed, were to prove vital ingredients for success: a place that serves drinks or food to the public must stand out thanks to its advantageous location, the beauty of the decoration, and the quality of its products. Le Procope had all three. As for the location, Procopio opened his café on rue des Fossés-Saint-Germain (today rue de l'Ancienne Comédie), opposite the Théâtre Français where Molière's close successors regularly played. For the decor, he made the rooms large and covered the floor with black and white tiles (which are still there today), ensuring a high standard of cleanliness. He increased the impression of space still further by hanging mirrors on the walls, which at that time were usually seen only in private houses and aristocratic mansions. The ceilings were lit with pendant crystal chandeliers, reflecting light from the candle flames. In short, opposite the Théâtre Français he created another stage, quite as elegant, where spectators could continue to suspend their disbelief, drinking not only coffee but syrupy wines: "rossoli" and "populo" were made from eau-de-vie, cloves, black pepper, coriander seeds, green anise, and sugar, heated to a syrup. Sorbets and all sorts of lemonades were also available. Aristocratic ladies would stop their carriages just in front of Le Procope and be served without having to set foot in the establishment, while the gentlemen crowded inside.

The café became a fashionable place where one could buy *nouvelles à la main*, the forerunner of the modern newspaper. Authors, actors, foppish peers, and lay abbots from the court were regular customers. Throughout the eighteenth century, at one time or other, one might have bumped into the country's most celebrated philosophers and writers such as Alembert, Diderot, Piron, and Jean-Jacques Rousseau. Voltaire set his comedy *L'Écossaise,* also known as *Le Caffé,* at Le Procope, and Beaumarchais held the first night party for *The Marriage of Figaro* there. During the Revolution, having undergone a change of ownership and name, as Café Zoppi, the coffee house become the unofficial headquarters of the Club des Cordeliers, the radical political group led successively by Danton, Marat, and Hébert.

With the Revolution also came an end to certain corporative restrictions, and the *cafés-limonadiers,* coffee houses such as Le Procope, were at last allowed to serve food. A contemporary account from 1807

notes that "nearly all today offer a light dinner, typically cutlets, kidneys in champagne wine, &c." The café had evolved into a restaurant, which would continue to attract artists and intellectuals throughout the nineteenth century. Enough of the original Procope still remains to give a good impression of this central point of Parisian social life: the black and white floor tiles, the fine mirrors on the ground floor, and the balcony from which authors and actors, fresh from their triumph at the Théâtre Français, would come and take one more curtain call from their public. As for the rest, having been freely refitted over the centuries, the restaurant today bears the traces of its successive occupants, from Voltaire's regular table, to the 1830 wallpapers depicting La Grande Révolution, and portraits of a diverse family, from Benjamin Franklin to poet Paul Verlaine. The food is classic *cuisine bourgeoise*, and the signature dish, coq au vin ivre de Juliénas, is mentioned as early as 1746 in Menon's classic work of the same name (but without the tagliatelle). Today, a clientele of good-natured tourists has replaced the intellectual heavyweights of days gone by.

The history of the restaurant as such really begins in Paris in 1782, with the opening of a luxurious establishment called La Grande Taverne de Londres in the Galerie de Valois next to the Palais-Royal. Antoine Beauvilliers, the proprietor, was the former *chef de bouche* (master of the household) to the Count of Provence, who was the king's brother and later became Louis XVIII. The birth of the restaurant was not, then, as persistent legend would have it, triggered by the Revolution, when chefs to the nobility were turned out onto the streets. The restaurant is an invention of the ancien régime, even if the social upheaval of the Revolution gave it a fundamental impetus. Brillat-Savarin's *La Physiologie du goût* tells us that Beauvilliers "was one of the first to have an elegant dining room, well-turned-out boys, a well-kept cellar and kitchen;" in a word, what would later be called a restaurant. Significantly, he placed great importance on the quality of service and surroundings. And Beauvilliers himself was no greasy-aproned cook: as an officer of the crown—a fact for which he was imprisoned in 1791—he greeted his customers wearing his sword.

The word *restaurant* itself refers back to another tradition: that of the "*bouillon restaurant*," a restorative soup, in which the word *restaurant* denotes the revitalizing virtues of consommé. In 1765, a certain Boulanger set up a few tables in his shop in rue des Poulies near the Louvre, serving predominantly working-class customers, judging by the individual portions of lambsfeet with chicken sauce. It was a precursor of the bistros of today. Yet restaurants did not really take off in Paris until the nineteenth century: in 1824, Brillat-Savarin still felt it necessary to furnish a job-description of the restaurateur: "he whose business consists in offering to the public a feast which is always ready, and

LE GRAND VÉFOUR

Underneath the arches of the Palais-Royal (facing page), Le Grand Véfour is the last survivor of the many establishments that animated these public gardens at the center of Parisian life between 1786 and 1829. A period sideboard, and tableware to harmonize with the historic setting (below). The main room of the restaurant with the red bench seats where Colette and Cocteau used to sit (following page).

whose dishes are made into portions at a fixed price at the request of the customers […]. What they call *carte*: an itemized list of the dishes, indicating their price, and *carte à payer*: the bill of the quantity of dishes provided and their prices."

But let us return to Beauvilliers. In the wake of his success, other establishments opened in the vicinity of the Palais-Royal, which was at that time one of the busiest parts of the capital. Instead of the rather inert gardens of today, during the eighteenth century the site was densely packed with wooden stalls selling all manner of Parisian merchandise, from fabric and clothes to jewelry and books. The alleyways between bustled with men and women looking for bargains, or perhaps a romantic adventure (Bonaparte made his first conquest there). And the site was effectively

immune to the forces of law and order: the Palais-Royal belonged to Louis-Philippe d'Orléans, grandson of the prince regent and therefore close enough to the king to be off limits to the local watch and the police. Under this extraterritorial arrangement, there was an upsurge in the circulation of satirical pamphlets and more or less clandestine gazettes, and the gardens were transformed into a hub for prostitution.

By 1789, the Palais-Royal was also one of the political hotbeds of the burgeoning Revolution. In the galleries surrounding the gardens, cafés, casinos, and taverns were opened, including the Café de Foy in the Galerie de Montpensier, the Café du Caveau and the Café de Chartres (to which we shall return in due course) in the Galerie de Beaujolais, and the Café Favier and the Café Méchanique in the Galerie de Valois. Beauvilliers' creation sounded the starting pistol for the restaurant race. Le Véry and Les Trois Frères Provençaux opened in the Galerie de Beaujolais, Le Petit Véfour in the Galerie de Valois, and the cafés were not slow to catch onto the new fashion and start serving food, too.

The Café de Chartres is one such example. Under the name of one of its first proprietors, Jean Véfour, the establishment attracted a refined foreign clientele after the royal Bourbon family returned to Paris in 1814. Count Rostopchin, the Moscow fire-raiser, was seen there dining with his French teacher, the beautiful Flore from the Théâtre des Variétés; the explorer Humboldt also dined there, invariably on "a vermicello, a breast of mutton and a bean." Since then, Le Grand Véfour (the *Grand* was added around 1825 to make the distinction from Le Petit Véfour) has always shone out in the gastronomic firmament, despite the decision of the future King Louis-Philippe in 1829 to clear the gardens of the stalls and drive out the prostitutes, after which the Palais-Royal was deserted. Le Grand Véfour withstood wind and tide, prompting a benevolent critic to say in 1842: "We go to Véfour's and we keep going back; the place will be there for as long as there are large appetites: you see that it is eternal." And this does appear to be true: no other Parisian establishment can claim to trace the genealogy of its chefs back over more than two hundred years.

LE GRAND VÉFOUR
The fine Pompeian-style reverse-painted glass panels are difficult to date, but they indicate the sumptuousness of this restaurant, which has always been a luxury establishment (facing page). The small dining room on the first floor is ideal for sequestered meetings (above).

LE GRAND VÉFOUR

Guy Martin is the latest in an uninterrupted line of great Parisian chefs spanning two centuries (above). An allegory of Autumn in a sensuous and calm climate (facing page).

After a brief eclipse due to the decline of the Palais-Royal, the gastronomic torch was taken up again after World War II. Louis Vaudable, then head of Maxim's, worked with Raymond Oliver, the greatest French chef of the 1950s, to bring the restaurant back up to scratch. The renaissance was rewarded in 1953 with three Michelin stars, and is continued today by Guy Martin, who has successfully maintained the standing of Le Grand Véfour, the ultimate witness of the eighteenth-century origins of the Parisian restaurant.

Inside this historic monument, the date of the interior decoration is still a matter of debate. Is this, as the profusion of Romanesque details might suggest, and as has long been believed, an example of Empire style? Or do we side with the authors of a report that led to Le Grand Véfour being listed as a historic monument in 1964, who held that only the ceiling, with its decorative grotesques, dates from the end of the eighteenth century? According to the report, the glazed canvases on the walls of the two dining rooms are in fact from the 1850s, when the Pompeian style came back into fashion. Were these panels imported from Italy, as some connoisseurs think, given their resemblance to those in the Café Florian in Venice, or are they to be attributed to Charles Prud'hon, a painter who was active under the Empire? None of this can be quite certain in the absence of documents formally establishing the provenance of the decor—but it doesn't really matter. We can all agree on the charm of these slightly erotic figures, allegories of diverse activities more or less closely related to the "art of the table," which create a unique atmosphere, both magical and timeless. Le Grand Véfour is clearly a place devoted to pleasure. Luckily, the quality of the food still matches the height of its beauty, allowing guests to unhitch themselves from the contemporary world for an evening and have a truly poetic experience. Guy Martin's preparations are perfect for this: his menus are modern without being unsettling. He has managed to preserve some of the great classics that made the reputation of Raymond Oliver (notably Pigeon Rainier III), but also proposes seductive culinary innovations with all the allure of a timeless classic—for example, his flavorsome oxtail with truffles.

The German philosopher Walter Benjamin wrote that Paris was "the capital of the nineteenth century," meaning the leading cultural city. This superiority was particularly marked in the area of gastronomy. Just flicking through Honoré de Balzac's *The Human Comedy,* or plunging into Gustave Flaubert's great Parisian novel *A Sentimental Education,* one can see the importance of restaurants at the time in the social life of the capital. The names of the Café Anglais, Frascati, Tortoni, but also Le Rocher de Cancale, the facade of which can still be seen on rue Montorgueil, turn up with significant frequency.

The Café Anglais—also visited by Emile Zola's heroine Nana—seems to have occupied the same position on the Parisian world map that would later be taken up by the Brasserie Lipp or Maxim's. It was here, on the corner of the boulevard des Italiens and rue Marivaux, next to the Opéra Comique, that Adolphe Dugléré, the inventor of the eponymous sole dish, made his reputation. The gourmet spirit of the place lives on today at La Tour d'Argent, whose founder, André Terrail, married the daughter of the last proprietor of the Café Anglais, Claudius Burdel, and inherited the contents of its prestigious cellars. Before the café itself closed in 1913, Marcel Proust was a regular customer. *In Search of Lost Time* can be read as a synthesis of the French nineteenth-century novel, and indeed a recasting of the mold—and it includes a detailed directory of the restaurants of the time. Thus in *Swann's Way,* the lovelorn hero finds refuge at one of most prestigious gastronomic addresses in Paris:

> On some days, instead of staying at home, he would go for luncheon to a restaurant not far off
> to which he had once been attracted by the excellence of its cookery, but to which he now went
> only for one of those reasons, at once mystical and absurd, which people call "romantic;"
> because this restaurant (which, by the way, still exists) bore the same name as the street in
> which Odette lived: La Pérouse.

LAPÉROUSE

Wide open onto the quai des Grands-Augustins, the facade of Lapérouse is authentically eighteenth century, as illustrated by the elegant wrought-iron balcony (above). The ground-floor dining room looks onto the Seine (facing page).

LAPÉROUSE

The Third Republic (1870–1940) lives on in this room on the first floor, particularly in the glass dividers engraved with stylized leaves and flowers.

Lapérouse, which does indeed still exist, provides a pretty good idea of what a grand nineteenth-century restaurant was like. You wouldn't go there just to eat. Business meetings and romantic trysts would be made there, and while some went with the intention of showing themselves off, for others the attraction was the possibility of *not* being seen. Lapérouse had private offices and rooms that could be locked from the inside, and a hidden exit onto the rue des Grands-Augustins. Guests were warned of imminent interruption by a bell placed directly on the steps of the service staircase, and could indulge in their favorite vices with complete peace of mind. What was more, since a clause in the French Civil Code classed restaurants as public places, illicit couples were protected from laws against adultery, and in particular the procedures pertaining to *in flagrante delicto*. When Lapérouse appeared on the Parisian landscape at the turn of the 1840s, its minimally decorated rooms were not yet accommodating prostitutes, merely their pimps whose girls were close on hand at the nearby Marché de la Vallée. Hidden from prying eyes, they would come and shake on deals, exchange rolls of gold coin, and drink to future business.

Jules Lapérouse bought the establishment in 1878, just as the Third Republic was being formed. It is to this astute proprietor that we owe the mounted canvases in the dining rooms, bearing idealized views of the preceding century. Throughout the restaurant, the walls were covered with leather embossed with Renaissance flower motifs, vaguely reminiscent of an inn in Dumas' *The Three Musketeers*. This pastiche style pleased the rich and influential of the time. Lapérouse became the place where members of the Senate would take their beautiful mistresses, who (as legend has it) would test the authenticity of the diamonds given them by their lovers by checking their sparkle in the mirrors.

The gastronomical standard was raised with the arrival in 1907 of a great chef, Marius Topolinski, at just the period when Proust sets the tortured affair between Swann and Odette de Crécy. Creations of his such as Prince Orloff veal chops, and Gratin de langoustines Georgette, have immortalized their creator just as they have the customers that inspired them. When Topolinski's son Roger bought the establishment

LAPÉROUSE

The small private rooms that made the fortune of Lapérouse: here guests could meet secretly for clandestine romantic affairs (above and facing page).

LE RELAIS PLAZA

Authentic 1930s decor at this brasserie in the fashion district. Above the bar, a fresco by F. Saqui depicts Diana the hunter in typically Art Deco style (below).

ALAIN DUCASSE

Alain Ducasse has turned the restaurant at the Plaza Athénée into one of the most prestigious tables in Paris. The interior designer Patrick Jouin recently lightened the feel of this slightly solemn room by hanging a chandelier with several hundred glass drops (facing page).

in 1923, the first Michelin Guides lavished it with praise. Topo, as he was called, was a gentle, bearded giant, a courteous host, and of course the soul of discretion. He was the personification of the idea that the setting should be as important as what goes onto the table. The Aga Khan, the Begum, and the Duke and Duchess of Windsor would come and slum it in this stronghold of Parisian society highlife. Lapérouse only lost its stars in 1969, when the fashion for nouvelle cuisine put more innovative chefs into the limelight. When its gentleman proprietor died, the restaurant sank slowly into a state of torpor from which it has not yet roused itself. Now the only regulars are staunch nostalgics and those to whom the notion of secrecy is still important, in a world dedicated to the celebration of media openness. One of the last clients of distinction was the former President François Mitterrand, who found shelter there when dining tête-à-tête with his illegitimate daughter Mazarine.

The experience of dining at a luxury hotel in Paris was, for a long time, characterized by pretentious service and a "catch-all" approach to the food. Naturally, the cuisine was based on the principles set out by Auguste Escoffier, but it seemed to have undergone a deliberate removal of flavor, so as not to offend the bland palates of international guests. While the Ritz and the Meurice were examples of this tendency in France, they never came to the highest recognition. In the 1930s, the Plaza Athénée made a popular departure into the realms of the luxury brasserie, with the Relais Plaza. This was a *grill*—a steakhouse—decorated in the most elegant style of the period, a sort of terrestrial luxury ocean liner. It was adopted by both the fashion and music worlds of Paris, being located in Avenue Montaigne, and not far from the Théâtre des Champs-Élysées. But the large, cold kitchens of the top Parisian hotels like the George V, continued to pride themselves on a readiness to satisfy their clients' every whim, even the most eccentric (an American guest at the George V once ordered, and was served, lobster in chocolate sauce). The Parisians were not interested.

Two great chefs reversed this terrible state of affairs, and their influence persuaded the grand hotels in Paris to equip themselves with chefs and a supporting brigade of staff that were worthy of the name. Christian Constant, originally from the southwest, introduced more stimulating tastes at the Ritz and then at the Crillon in the 1980s, bringing rough-and-ready dishes to tables that hitherto had seen little more than upgraded room service. This affected a whole generation of young chefs—including Yves Camdeborde at the Régalade and Thierry Breton at Chez Michel—who swarmed into Paris, finding places in other luxury hotels and neo-bistros during the checkered-tablecloth boom of the 1990s. The second chef to restore nobility to the grand hotels was, of course, Alain Ducasse.

Following in Escoffier's footsteps in 1987, he took over the Louis XV at the Hôtel de Paris in Monaco. He was a disciple of Alain Chapel and Roger Vergé, and came to be regarded as the top chef of his generation, thanks to his inspired reinvention of Mediterranean cuisine. Then he headed up to Paris and started collecting Michelin stars. He made the restaurant of the Plaza Athénée one of the finest in the capital. The other luxury hotels were not long in following his lead.

The Meurice was once a regular meeting place for the English in Paris. This establishment, created in 1835 by Augustin Meurice, a postmaster from Calais whose stagecoach line terminated near the rue de Rivoli, is the earliest of the grand hotels in Paris. At the turn of the last century, a thorough renovation gave it a patina of the *ancien régime* that it still has today. The restaurant is more evocative of a ballroom than a dining room, with its medallion-backed armchairs, crystal chandeliers, two fine marble chimneys facing each other, its ceiling painted with a very Tiepolo-like fresco, its romantic and vaguely mythological paintings, and the walls adorned with stucco, gilded wood, and mock-marble columns. Until the 1940s, one could also be served on the roof garden terrace on the first floor, which was reached by an elevator decorated as a reproduction of Marie-Antoinette's sedan chair. Marcel Proust, Salvador Dalí, and Florence Gould and her circle of writer friends—Marcel Jouhandeau, Paul Léautaud, and Paul Morand—often came to this sumptuous and slightly kitsch place. A certain whiff of decadence hung around the Meurice for a long time, partly because of the presence of German staff headquarters here during the Occupation in World War II. Its rebirth was all the more spectacular for that.

In 2003, the young Yannick Alleno, who had distinguished himself at the Hôtel Scribe, took over the running of the kitchens and straightaway earned two Michelin stars for the Meurice. His multifaceted cuisine, simultaneously inventive and respectful of tradition, dazzled the Parisian food critics. This is a chef capable of masterfully reinterpreting a classic dish like lièvre à la royale by combining the two competing recipes, that of Sénateur Couteaux and the version preferred by Carême. And at the same time he can play in the contemporary register with disconcerting ease: take his Balik salmon with potato crust, leek custard and caviar, which manages to be both light and hearty at the same time. Yannick Alleno's talent and virtuosity have brought a regular Parisian clientele to the Meurice, and their allegiance to the place is itself a sign of quality for visitors.

Unlike the Meurice, the Hôtel de Crillon is a true period piece, built behind the colonnade erected in 1758 by Gabriel on the place de la Concorde. In the beginning, this magnificent private mansion was intended to accommodate ambassadors to foreign countries, which explains the name of its restaurant, Les Ambassadeurs. The sumptuous eighteenth-century residence came into the hands of the

LE MEURICE
Hurried or uninformed customers might take the Louis XV decor for genuine work of the mid-eighteenth century, but its marble columns and chandeliers (facing page), paneled mirrors, and Sedan chair at the entrance (below) are pure early twentieth century creations.

LES AMBASSADEURS

Les Ambassadeurs has inherited all the splendor of the Hôtel de Crillon's former ballroom, where it is situated: marble floor, marble walls, and large Venetian mirrors.

Crillon family, descendants of one of Henry IV's favorites, after the Revolution, and they lived there until they sold it to the Société des Hôtels du Louvre in 1907. It was not, then, until last century that the Crillon became the grand, luxurious hotel we know today, appropriately enough fulfilling the function it was originally intended for: the accommodation of distinguished guests.

Because of its proximity to the Élysée Palace, the Crillon is still a regular port of call for the minister of foreign affairs, who has visiting heads of state stay there. The crystal chandeliers, marble statues, and wall mirrors give a timeless feel, but there are subtle touches to bring the setting up to date: champagne-colored curtains play with the light from the place de la Concorde; armchairs and tables have been given a new lease of life by lighter colors, harmonizing well with shades in the marble. In the evening, the monumental chandeliers shine with all their might, while the wall lights give a more diffuse glow.

Jean-François Piège, who came to the Crillon with a large part of the staff from the Plaza Athénée, has been inspired by this eighteenth-century atmosphere to offer cuisine with pomp and ceremony, but cleverly modernized. The presentation does suffer somewhat from the choice of tableware, which is just too "designer" not to clash with the setting, but this affectation is outweighed by Piège's signature dishes. The Ossetra caviar with full-flavored aromatic broth and Dublin Bay prawns, the Bresse chicken, the crayfish with morels and onions, and the strawberry vacherin with childrens' strawberry candies and basil, were perfected by this great culinary technician when he was the principal associate of Alain Ducasse. As at the Meurice, two Michelin stars rewarded the skill of this chef, still young, but already a master.

A stone's throw from the Crillon, in rue Royale, stands Maxim's, a one-stop incarnation of a certain idea of Paris. The singer Serge Gainsbourg, in a rather forgotten song, summed up the atmosphere like this: "*Ah! baiser la main d'une femme du monde, et m'écorcher les lèvres à ses diamants, et puis dans*

LES AMBASSADEURS
All the accoutrements of traditional service: dessert trolley, champagne bowl, and valuable crystal glasses and silverware (facing page and above).

The stained-glass ceiling reflected in Art Nouveau mirrors. The glass wall lamps throw a diffuse brightness over the single most emblematic place in the City of Lights (facing page and below).

la Jaguar, brûler son léopard avec une cigarette anglaise et s'envoyer des dry au Gordon et des Pimm's Number One avant que de filer chez Maxim's, grand seigneur dix sacs au chasseur!" ("Ah, to kiss the hand of a fine lady, and scratch my lips on her diamonds, then in the Jaguar, burn her leopard-skin coat with an English cigarette and down some Gordon's and vermouth and Pimm's Number One before zooming off to Maxim's, feeling generous, a hundred francs to the doorman!") All the elements of the myth are there: the Maxim's doorman with his smart red uniform, the diamond-digging dame, and the anglophile snobbery which is so typically Parisian—which we also see in the restaurant's name, anglicized by the first proprietor, Maxime Gaillard, supposedly to add polish. There is an element of timelessness, too: instead of rolling up in a horse-drawn carriage like his illustrious predecessors, Gainsbourg screeches up to the door in an E-type Jag, showing how in the 1960s, Maxim's still embodied the temptation to live life at its fastest.

The place has settled somewhat as it has grown in international fame. With all the flexibility allowed by that name's mythical association with Paris as a constantly fizzing City of Light, Maxim's is now used by Pierre Cardin almost as a brand name. In a sense, the name has come to be separated from the place. There are now Maxim's plates, champagne, chocolates, cigars, and even Maxim's scent, not to mention the other establishments opened under the name in Monte-Carlo, New York, Beijing, and Shanghai. The great fashion designer is no ordinary restaurateur; perhaps a figure of this caliber was just what was needed to help Maxim's weather the years.

The facade, the series of three rooms inside linked by the famous Omnibus bar (today on the first floor), the mezzanine, and the small saloons are Art Nouveau, dating exactly from the turn of the century. But this is a "flamboyant" Art Nouveau: the architect Louis Marnez favored eccentric scrollwork, exuberant organic motifs, mahogany woodwork picked out with copper, and wall seats and armchairs covered with red leather. The sumptuous display is given further complexity by mirrors that catch reflections of nymphs (frescoes by Martens and Soulié), semi-translucent stained-glass windows, built up in overlapping layers in the style of Emile Gallé, and the glass roof of the large dining room where lemon tree branches intertwine.

The patrons themselves were no less flamboyant, and helped secure Maxim's international reputation. For it was no genteel clientele, even if crowned heads, writers, and artists were regularly present. The patrons one came to see—or to be seen with—at Maxim's in the 1900s were the *belles horizontales*, professional beauties with the names of princesses: Émilienne d'Alençon, Liane de Pougy, Caroline Otero. They reigned supreme over the Paris demimonde and

their scandalous goings-on added spice to many a dinner at rue Royale. In this sense, Maxim's is more of a theater than a restaurant, and its inventor, Eugène Cornuché, more of a theater director than a restaurateur. The rivalry between the beautiful Otero and Liane de Pougy has entered into legend. The former appeared one evening at Maxim's festooned with jewels that she had finessed out of the Grand Duke Nicholas, like so many flags brought back from a victorious Russian campaign. She paraded at length in the Omnibus bar to establish her superiority. But the brilliance of her trophies paled when her rival made an even more spectacular entrance. Liane de Pougy, in a light, simple, white dress that set off her beauty, was followed by none other than her maid, walking three paces behind her, clad in her precious stones and looking like a lavish shop window at Christmas time. The upstart triumphed, and the columns of *Le Figaro*, which carried an account of this civil war, were in tumult.

Several figures contributed to the metamorphosis of Maxim's into a mythological temple. First there was Albert, or *Monsieur* Albert, the "maitre d' to princes, and prince of maitre d's." From 1931–59, this stickler for custom maintained a list of clients that ran like a *Who's Who* of high society. He sat guests according to strict notions of precedence, from the best tables at the front, to the back of the back room, as if organizing ambassadors for an audience with the king.

Then came the Vaudable dynasty, the father Octave, the son Louis, and his wife, who transformed this restaurant little by little into a business of many parts, on which Pierre Cardin only had to affix his mark. Has this caused Maxim's to lose its soul? Certainly, what was at the hub of Parisian society has become one of the places most frequently visited by busloads of tourists. But Pierre Cardin still holds private parties there, which are very popular with the fashion world. At the heart of the capital, despite the franchise, Maxim's still continues to exert its fascination.

MAXIM'S

The restaurant on rue Royale is reminiscent of a boudoir in its spectacular, muffled intimacy. The theory of unity of decoration, so important to the supporters of Art Nouveau, is expressed here in all its coherence (above). The first-floor bar where Pierre Cardin still gives sumptuous Parisian parties once a month (facing page).

LUCAS CARTON

*Lucas Carton before
the renovation undergone in
2005 at the hands of Noé
Duchaufour-Lawrance, the
designer of Sketch in London.
One might prefer the discreet
coherence of the 1900 decor to
the post-historic audacity of the
new millennium. Yet the bulk of
the protected, historic interior
remains, and is visible to the
guests (above and facing page).*

A little further up the rue Royale, on the corner of Place de la Madeleine and Boulevard Malesherbes, is a much more discreet facade than Maxim's. It conceals another Art Nouveau jewel, which contrasts in its sobriety and elegance with the exaggerated profusion of its famous neighbor. Lucas Carton is today one of the most sought-after tables in Paris. The reason lies in the presence in the kitchen of Alain Senderens, one of the three musketeers of nouvelle cuisine, with Michel Guérard and Jean and Pierre Troisgros (who count as one). Senderens conquered Paris at the Archestrate in the 1970s, before finding a setting at Lucas Carton to match his cuisine. This wonderful chef has an acute sense of harmony, and has always had an ability to marry the richness of his ingredients with a lightness of preparation, and match the finesse of great wines with the complexity of his dishes' flavors.

Harmony is exactly the impression you get when you enter this restaurant. Before passing through the double doors, admire the Art Nouveau facade by the architect Étienne de Gounevitch. Once over the threshold, prepare to be charmed by the decor, which is bare without being austere; sensuous without being ostentatious. It was probably designed under the direction of the cabinetmaker Louis Majorelle, one of the leading lights of the École de Nancy, which was at the height of its popularity at that time. Between 1904 and 1905, craftsmen such as the sculptor Planel, cabinetmakers from the firm of Lucas & Co., and the bronzesmith Galli set their hands to this concerto in sycamore and maple. The blond tones of the organic motifs produce a soothing effect, as do the bronze wall lights representing female heads emerging from flower stems, framed by three luminous irises. Furnishings of an equally high quality—a clock, a sideboard, a credence table, and a chest—blend with the setting. The original paintings have been replaced by large mirrors, reflecting this gentleness harmoniously.

Lucas Carton has always been a temple of good form, ever since 1732, when a certain Robert Lucas from Great Britain founded a Taverne de Londres in rue Boissy-d'Anglas. In the nineteenth century it became the Taverne Lucas, then the Taverne de France, then from 1925 was transformed into the reputable establishment it has been ever since, by the dedication (and the name) of Francis Carton. Carton had worked at the Café Anglais and the Maison Dorée, and was president of both the Company of Paris Cooks and the World Federation of Cooks, the two concerns apparently being all but identical in that day. The Goncourt brothers were regulars, and Richard Wagner ate there every evening when he was in Paris composing *Die Meistersinger*. The upper echelons of the business world liked to meet in the private rooms on the first floor, which assured the most complete confidentiality thanks to a private entrance from passage de la Madeleine.

LUCAS CARTON

The woodwork is listed as a historic monument, and has thankfully been left untouched in the "new" Lucas Carton.

LUCAS CARTON

The organic forms of Art Nouveau express a discreet sensuality: flower-women and fragile dragonflies engraved on the glass screens inhabit the mysterious arabesques of the woodwork (facing page and above).

Francis Carton belonged to that class of chefs who have perpetuated the tradition of great French cuisine. His sole de la Tante Marie, his lobster gratin, and his woodcock flambé earned him the highest honors from the *Michelin Guide*, on the insistence of customers who were members of the 1912 Club des Cent, which included industrialists, politicians, and publishers with a mission to promote "good old French Cooking." Carton was also honored as *chef attitré*—chef by appointment—to the Third Republic. After the war, Carton's son-in-law and daughter took over the business, but were unable to maintain its standards. It was only in 1985, when Alain Senderens got behind the stove, that the establishment again reached the gastronomic splendor without which the upper echelons of Parisian society cannot imagine doing business. With this clientele from the smartest neighborhoods, and with this setting, Senderens, the quiet revolutionary of nouvelle cuisine, had to find a new angle. This he did, with gusto, by reviving an ancient recipe, canard Apicius, named after the great Roman compiler of *De Re Coquinaria*. But his hallmark is to provide the ideal glass of wine to complement each dish on the menu. In 2005 he decided to "give back" his three Michelin stars and offer simpler fare at more accessible prices. The style is to be rejuvenated, and a new look superimposed onto the old one. Paris will vote with its feet.

"Oh, oysters! I've been simply longing for some!" exclaims Albertine, the narrator's beloved in *In Search of Lost Time,* on hearing the cry of a passing oyster-seller. Proust's rejoinder to his character's remark is as unexpected as it is significant: "she would find better oysters at Prunier's." It could be an advertising slogan of the time. Prunier's restaurant was started in 1872 from the meeting of two late nineteenth-century archetypes: a cellarman in charge of choosing and bottling wine, and the governess of a mansion. Alfred Prunier was from Normandy. He worked in a bistro on rue Montholon and knew just as much about seafood as he did about wine. Catherine Virion was from Lorraine, and had worked for the chief rabbi in

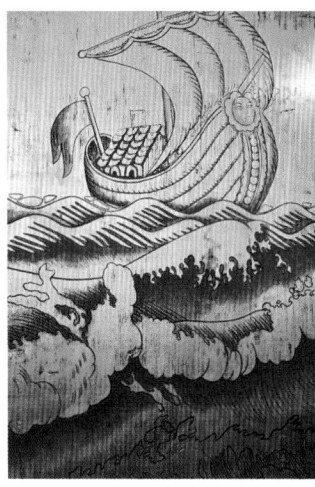

PRUNIER

From within a Russian
isba *theme, Jacques Grange's*
panels on the first floor
(above left) echo the gold
and copper tones of the metal
panels downstairs, which mark
out the different stages
of an evening at Prunier
(above right and facing page).

Paris, then for Princess Dolgorouki. She was a good manager and a cordon-bleu cook. Together, they opened a restaurant—a first step on the social ladder for these two from the provinces—first on rue d'Antin, then on rue Duphot, near La Madeleine, which is the one Proust refers to in his novel. This restaurant still exists today under the name of Goumard, but its Art Nouveau interior designed by Louis Majorelle has been pretty badly damaged (although the toilets are still much admired, their proportions, apparently, prompting Charles de Gaulle to say that they were "equal to my standing").

Prunier quickly became the supplier of seafood to the smartest buyers in Paris, who included at the time aristocrats from the Faubourg-Saint-Germain, English lords, American millionaires, and Russian grand dukes, in more or less equal measure. The Franco–Russian alliance of 1892 launched the Parisian fashion for caviar. Émile Prunier, heir to the restaurant's founders, introduced tanks, in imitation of the Norwegian fish markets, from which live fish could be sold. The typhoid epidemic of 1906 was rumored to have been caused by the consumption of raw oysters; Émile Prunier, as founder of the Oyster Culture Trade Union, helped to get new sanitary procedures adopted to guarantee the quality and harmlessness of the French produce. When the Bolshevik Revolution cut Russia off from the rest of the world, Prunier took steps to ensure an independent supply of caviar, and invested in sturgeon fishing in the Gironde. In 1924 this enterprising man also designed new premises on avenue Victor Hugo in the sixteenth arrondissement, which he intended to be ultra-modern. This was the Prunier-Traktir, *traktir* being an old Russian word for bistro. He died shortly after the restaurant was completed but his work lives on: for all Parisians, the name of Prunier remains unfailingly linked to all that comes from the sea.

The interior at Prunier was the work of Louis-Hippolyte Boileau, often confused with his father Louis-Charles, who designed the department store Bon Marché with Gustave Eiffel. Boileau, an eclectic architect if ever there was one, was also responsible for the wooden-framed pavilions for Togo and Cameroon in the Colonial Exhibition of 1931 in the Bois de Vincennes, which have since been transformed into a Buddhist temple. He also designed the monumental Palais de Chaillot, with Léon Azema and Jacques Carlu. Louis-Hippolyte Boileau was highly regarded by contemporaries for his interiors of bars and restaurants, which marked the beginning of the explosion of Art Deco into public spaces. The restaurants at the Hôtel Lutétia, the Grand Café de Madrid, and Bon Marché are examples of his work. His masterpiece, however, remains Prunier's restaurant, where he headed a team of leading artists and craftsmen: the artist Léon Carrière, the glass engraver Paul Binet, the sculptor Pierre Le Bourgeois, the leather engraver Alexeï Brodowitz, and

the mosaicist Auguste Labouret. The latter's facade is enticing: a precursor of block stained-glass work set in cement, seen more often in religious settings. Here it illustrates the theme of the sea in blue-green tones, picked out with very Art Deco geometrical hoops. Inside, the marine atmosphere is to be found in the floor, punctuated with white lozenges encrusted in black marble, and in gold circle motifs on the walls, which evoke the play of champagne bubbles. Inlaid onyx and glass give the mosaics an oriental feel. Pleasingly oversimplified panels by Pierre Le Bourgeois—golden metal openwork on wood—mark out the different stages leading from the bar to your table, like so many stations. Glass engravings with geometric motifs reminiscent of waves give an ethereal character to the whole interior. On the tables, the octagonal plates, designed with controlled abstraction by the painter Mathurin Méheut in 1932, evoke fantastical views of Brittany. Some of the original fittings in a period that was already concerned about functional comfort are worthy of note: the heated handrail on the staircase, the natural cooling system for the seafood displayed in the window, and the gallant detail of hooks on the bar for ladies' handbags. Pierre Bergé, who bought the premises in 2001 (he now has shared ownership with Caviar House), added a room on the first floor decorated by Jacques Grange in the style of a Russian *isba*, the walls and panels covered with gold leaf and bearing sea themes, inspired by Ivan Bilibine's illustrations of Russian folk tales. As an establishment dedicated to the celebration of seafood and caviar, Prunier is a luxury version of another type of restaurant that Paris was first to lay claim to: the brasserie.

PRUNIER

The entrance of Prunier, with its mosaic facade and Art Deco sign, invites one on a journey where champagne and seafood have their part to play (above). The elegant staircase, with a detail that sums up a whole era: discreet lighting under the handrail (facing page).

Brasseries

On Tap

The definition of *brasserie* given by Paul-Émile Littré in his 1877 *Dictionnaire de la langue française,* is a "place where beer is sold by the measure and where there are only benches and wooden tables." Yet at precisely the period when the great lexicographer was compiling his work, refugees were coming to Paris from Alsace, after that province had been annexed by Prussia, and opening establishments called *brasseries* that exhibited quite a different standard of comfort from that suggested by Littré's definition. The newfound predilection for beer in the capital dates from slightly earlier on, however, before the terrible defeat of the French in the Franco–Prussian war. It was the Paris–Strasbourg railway, inaugurated by Napoleon III on July 17, 1851, which first brought Alsatian businessmen into the capital in number, and with them came the firm intention of offering the Parisian public a type of rapid refreshment hitherto unseen: sauerkraut and a glass of beer. Writers and artists such as Baudelaire, Corot, and Courbet practically lived in these popular and noisy places, where the city came as never before to show itself off.

The first beer pump was an Alsatian idea, and was installed in Paris in 1864 by Frédéric Bofinger in his brand new brasserie at the Bastille. The invention revolutionized the selling of beer and established it as a regular beverage with the working classes. The prospect of being served by young and pretty barmaids did no harm either: the *brasseries à femmes*—some of which tipped over into prostitution—were places where one could smoke, read the paper, and relax in a permissive atmosphere (which the temperance leagues were quick to condemn). Édouard Manet conveyed the joyous and quasi-erotic atmosphere of these places in a series of paintings and drawings begun in 1875.

Yet beer-drinking was still slow to gain popularity in Paris. Back in 1718 the German traveler Joachim Christoph Nemeitz had complained that the beer in Paris was unhealthy. "Hops," he wrote, "are often replaced by bitter herbs or by ox gall." But by the end of the nineteenth century, beer was definitely conquering the capital. The phylloxera epidemic had damaged the country's vineyards and made wine scarce and expensive. Also, the mere act of buying beer allowed Parisians to express a patriotic solidarity with the annexed province of Alsace. The authorities even looked on this low-alcohol drink benignly, as being much less harmful than the devastating absinthe. In a country of heavy drinkers, it was better that people become drunk on beer than on eau-de-vie or on its aniseed-flavored substitute. Everything conspired to give the brasseries a firm footing in the Parisian landscape, and they have never lost it.

BOFINGER

Art almost as far as the restrooms. Brasseries do not do things by halves when it comes to decor: the public of the time wanted their money's worth (below and facing page).

On the right bank of the Seine, near the Faubourg-Saint-Antoine, Bofinger has, over its one-hundred-and-fifty-year life, embodied the spirit of the political left. This has always been a politically active part of Paris, ever since the storming of the Bastille on July 14, 1789. Today the place de la Bastille and La Roquette, the area surrounding it, are among the more bohemian parts of Paris, inhabited by artists converting old furniture-makers' studios into loft apartments. Bofinger is one of their favorite meeting points; it owes much of its character to its local residents. One finds more real Parisians per table than tourists out for a good time.

The reputation as a "left-wing" brasserie is largely due to the assiduous patronage of the famous French politician Édouard Herriot. This great figure was as well known in the Soviet Union as in the United States—he met both Stalin and FD Roosevelt in the 1930s. When staying in Paris, he loved to repair to this plebeian atmosphere, and hold political meetings there. Édouard Herriot formed the Cartel des Gauches, the progressive political coalition that governed France from 1924–27 and from 1932–36 in room no. 9 on the first floor of Bofinger. The place has hardly changed; one can easily imagine that meeting of goateed sages, shoveling down the sauerkraut and beer and shrewdly reshaping the world. A great deal of politics at that time was conducted at the café-bar of the National Assembly, but more still on the benches at Bofinger's. Later, in 1981, after the victory of the Union de la Gauche, François Mitterrand sat on the same benches with his minister of culture, Jack Lang, and, realizing that the interior was not officially protected, took the decision to have it listed as a *lieu de mémoire*—a place of memory.

In fact, Bofinger has been connected with politics since it started. It is situated—as are so many brasseries—not far from a train station, one that has now disappeared, the Gare de la Bastille. It is also not far from two other important termini, the Gare de Lyon and the Gare d'Austerlitz, which are in effect the gateways to the southwest and southeast of France. The parliamentary representatives and senators, coming up from their districts to attend the National Assembly, meet there almost as a matter of course. Especially since the modest premises at no. 5, rue de la Bastille, once distinguished only by the generosity of the beer pump, were enlarged in 1919. Frédéric Bofinger's successors, his son-in-law Albert Bruneau, and Louis Barraud, bought nos. 3 and 7 on either side and began the process of renovation and improvement. The decor we see today dates from this period. It embodies the spirit of the Parisian brasserie: a happy mix of bench seats in buttoned leather, as if from a gentleman's club, Thonet bentwood chairs, and paneled mirrors surrounded with delicate

blind arcades. The retrospective style after the disaster of World War I seems to want to merge Art Nouveau with the later Belle Époque. The cupola dominating the large main room is decorated with floral motifs, which combine with the greenery on the ceramic vases and the white napkins on the tables to give a pastoral look, almost as if one were eating at a large inn. The sign at the entrance, depicting two figures in Alsatian folk costume, and the decoration in the room above, are by the artist Hansi and date from 1930. In a naïve and fresh style, they evoke the idealized picture of Alsace that Paris wanted to believe at the time.

Now under the ownership of the Groupe Flo, who control the majority of Paris' brasseries, Bofinger is known and appreciated for its oyster display, its properly traditional *choucroute* (sauerkraut), and an atmosphere which owes a lot to the regular Parisian clientele who are attached to this legendary establishment.

It was in some ways inevitable that the brasserie started by another Alsatian, Léonard Lipp, in Saint-Germain-des-Prés in 1880, should become the intellectual heart of Paris. As the Brasserie des Bords du Rhin was starting up, the main publishers of contemporary French literature—Flammarion, Gallimard, Grasset, le Mercure de France, and others—were moving into the same neighborhood. The proximity of the major publishing houses quickly made the Brasserie Lipp a meeting place for writers and, following close on their heels, politicians (who typically in France undergo a struggle at some point in their lives with a repressed desire to become authors). Paris is in the center of France, and the Paris literati tend to consider themselves to be the center of the city. Little wonder then that Léon-Paul Fargue summed up the function of Lipp over the twentieth century like this: "Lipp is without a doubt one of those places, perhaps the only place, where one can get, for the price of a glass of beer, a complete and accurate political or

LIPP

Beneath the appearance of a simple brasserie, Lipp is a labyrinth of rank and reputation, where every table occupies a particular position in the hierarchy of the Parisian social elite (facing page). The beer glass on the shop front and the notice prohibiting the feeding of dogs are a reminder that Lipp, too, was once a working-class establishment (above).

LIPP

*The "right side" of Lipp,
where one goes to be seen
(above). The waiters are
numbered in order of seniority,
"un" being the one who
has been there longest
(facing page).*

intellectual summary of the day." Fargue wrote these lines in *Le Piéton de Paris* in 1932, but they remained true for as long as Saint-Germain-des-Prés retained its monopoly over French publishing life. To list the figures who have been seen at Lipp at one time or another would be to recite the history of contemporary French literature.

The precise degree of celebrity of guests at Lipp could always be gauged by the rigorous seating customs. Marcellin Cazes, who took over the establishment in 1920, quickly understood the value of a ceremonious approach, as did his son Roger, who ran it until 1987. On December 26, 1926, at a reopening banquet after some renovation work, Marcellin Cazes first put into operation the unwritten rules that would regulate the Brasserie Lipp with the precision of the court of Louis XIV for the next sixty years. Following an unshakable hierarchy, he sent strangers, tourists, and run-of-the-mill diners up to the first floor. For the other guests, their importance was directly proportional to the distance of their table from the terrace, and particularly from the front entrance. The B-list were herded into the second room, behind the cash desk, facing the vertiginous staircase that leads to the toilets. VIPs had the honor of being seated in the first room, which was decorated with ceramic panels by Léon Fargue (Léon-Paul Fargue's father) with designs of exotic plants and pretty friezes of macaws. The most important position, reserved for great stars and, when bestowed, worth a Prix Goncourt in its own way, was the table situated in the right angle just past the revolving door at the entrance, from where the lucky laureate could acknowledge those coming in, as might a host. The personalities of the affable yet inflexible Cazes contributed greatly to the renown of Lipp. They treated their role as chamberlains of the Paris smart set with the utmost seriousness; perhaps only those who have experienced at first hand negotiations for a table with these two potentates can realize just how important they judged their function to be.

The last twenty years have been less glorious for Lipp. Saint-Germain-des-Prés has had its literary day: several of the most important publishers have moved elsewhere, and the neighborhood has become distinctly gentrified. But loyal customers still come back to sample the unchanging classics on the menu: bœuf gros sel, poached haddock in beurre blanc, and a chateaubriand steak and fries which, for us, stands as the best in Paris—doubtless due to a childhood memory.

The English bar is a typically French concept. Parisian society has regularly been seized by Anglo-mania since the eighteenth century. In the 1880s, despite the colonial rivalry between the two powers, this feeling reached its height and was widely manifested in society, from elegant gentlemen's fashions to the adoption of "tea time." English bars flourished, and it was no accident that one of the first to open in Paris, in 1878, was located near the stock exchange, La Bourse. The top traders were quick to become regulars at Gallopin, and were followed there by aspiring brokers and dealers from the trading pit. English words etched on the front windows advertise "American Drinks" and a "Luncheon Bar." The gold letters running above proclaim, again in English, "Stock Exchange Luncheon Bar," leaving no doubt as to the establishment's intended function.

Gustave Gallopin married an English heiress, a member of the Wyborn family, who had made their fortune from grocery outlets. He started a fashion for cocktails, and served beer in small silver tankards (*gallopins,* named after himself) which are still in use today. For many years a large tin bath filled with water, ice, and bottles of champagne was kept at the ready to celebrate outstanding deals on the exchange. The current decor dates from 1886: the date is painted on the ceiling. The large bar and the Victorian-style paneling in all the rooms are made of Cuban mahogany and were supplied directly from London. The ceiling and wall lights, with their tulip-shaped glass shades, were worked out of copper by Parisian craftsmen, but seem to put the finishing touches to a very coherent look of Englishness. For the Exposition Universelle in 1900, Gustave Gallopin partitioned off the back room with a wall of opaline, decorated with Art Nouveau flowers and branches in translucent enamel. The design is reflected infinitely by a double mirror effect. In the summertime, this glass partition slides back to reveal a small garden. In the hands of the present owners, the Alexander family, who previously owned Bofinger and Lapérouse, Gallopin has been preserved in its original state. The stock exchange has long since left the neighborhood, but regular business customers still appreciate the traditional menu: seafood dishes, Andouillette de Troyes ("5A" grade, the best), or the chateaubriand with fresh green beans; and above all, the unchanging interior, a reminder for posterity of the financial trading quarter that Paris once had.

GALLOPIN

Dabblers in the stock exchange used to crowd into the English bar at Gallopin (facing page) to exchange hot tips. It remained a rendezvous for investors until the 1980s, when the Paris Bourse went completely electronic. The back room with its pretty 1900 glass partition (below). The acid-etched windows bear the ornamented initial of the proprietor, and modish English slogans (following pages).

Brasserie Mollard, opposite the Gare Saint-Lazare, has not had the glamorous history of Lipp, but it is worth a detour to see. First of all, it is one of the only large, historic brasseries in Paris not to be owned by the Groupe Flo. The pristine original interior makes it one of the most beautiful examples of the Parisian modern style. And it has, at least in part, preserved its original function: to refresh the hurried traveler before he embarks upon the formidable adventure of a railway journey.

Interestingly, the proprietors who first hung their sign here in 1865 were not from Alsace, but Savoie, a Monsieur and Madame Mollard. They were given a very cool reception by the Alsatian community in Paris. A contemporary competitor set up only two doors away, and is still there today: the Brasserie Jacqueminot Graff, better known as "Au roi de la bière." Here, everything—the gabled facade, with its alternating brick and half-timbers, the sculpted decoration of tankards on tables and a stork above its nest, and above all, at the center of the composition, the figure of Gambrinus, the folk hero of northern and eastern Europe (who is said to have invented beer after making a pact with the devil)—is supposed to suggest (in rather kitsch taste) a typical Alsace house, at least as it might be imagined by Parisians. By contrast, the Mollards renovated their premises in 1895, bringing the mosaic setter Enrico Bichi over from Italy, and giving overall control of the work to Édouard Niermans, the Art Nouveau architect. Niermans' later work includes the Rumpelmeyer tearooms on rue de Rivoli (which today is Angelina) and the Hôtel Negresco in Nice. The ceramic panels, made at Sarreguemines in the east of France, depict towns reached from Saint-Lazare—Deauville, Saint-Germain-en-Laye, Ville d'Avray—as well as the station itself. And of course there is the obligatory allegory of France's lost provinces: Alsace and Lorraine. One other picture is worthy of note in passing: it represents an orgy. A reminder of how, although this was just a passing place for many, the atmosphere could become steamy for the regulars.

MOLLARD

The mosaics at Mollard give this brasserie the feel of a Byzantine basilica, dedicated to pleasure (facing page and above).

MOLLARD

The stork fresco is less
"remember Alsace" than
"imagine Japan," very much
in the spirit of the 1900s.

LE TRAIN BLEU

There was a time when restaurants were cathedrals. The station buffet at the Gare de Lyon looks, in its way, like the sacristy of Saint Peter's in Rome: gilt, stucco work, huge paintings on the ceiling and walls. And the traveler was treated like a monsignor (above, facing, and following page).

The original wall decorations were hidden behind paint and tall mirrors in 1920, and thus miraculously preserved. They only emerged again in 1965, at the behest of the new proprietors, giving the Brasserie Mollard a freshness that is a great part of its charm. It remains busy, especially at midday with office workers from the surrounding businesses. In the evenings, travelers still break their journey here, while other interested parties are drawn by the authenticity of the place. Mollard serves characteristic brasserie fare. The seafood platters are particularly impressive, the excellent quality due to ingredients picked directly from seawater tanks on the premises. The Brasserie Mollard has been a listed building since 1989.

Of course the rapid development of the brasserie in Paris is linked to the expansion of the railways. And from this point of view, the inauguration at the Gare de Lyon of Le Train Bleu on April 7, 1901, during the Exposition Universelle, marks a kind of apotheosis. Some distinguished artists were involved in its creation, but what really marks out Le Train Bleu is the sheer excess of decoration. The Paris-Lyon-Marseille railway company clearly intended to make this a modern cathedral, dedicated to the celebration of the most up-to-date means of transport of the time. Their success could not be more vividly apparent.

The first impression, on pushing through the revolving doors from the station, is one of drowning in the exuberance of the sculpted plasterwork gleaming from the walls and ceilings. Then one notices the proportions of the main room: eighty-five feet long, with a ceiling of almost forty feet, lit by two superb crystal chandeliers. Wide windows, centered in archways, look directly out onto the street. Finally the eye settles on the frescoes that occupy all the remaining space available: the ceilings, the walls, and the spandrels between the arches. They depict landscapes from the Alps, the south of

France, Algeria, and Tunisia, as well as the three principal cities on the line, Paris, Lyon, and Marseille. To the right of this great room is another, the *Salle Dorée,* or Golden Room, almost as big and just as richly decorated. To the left are two more modestly proportioned dining areas that evoke Tunisia and Algeria respectively, the ceilings and walls ornamented with arabesques of a vaguely eastern style. Critics at the time made fun of this decorative profusion, dubbing it the "annual trade fair for landscape gardeners." But even if the undeniably pretentious style is not your cup of tea, you cannot but gasp at the pure indulgence of the site and the overall effect. Thirty painters took part in the collective composition, including Guillaume Dubuffe and Gaston Casimir Saint-Pierre,

LA COUPOLE

The oyster display (above). At La Coupole local artists are still invited to submit their works for temporary exhibition in the explosive hubbub of this immense former warehouse.

official celebrities of the École des Beaux-Arts at the time. Numerous sculptors, plasterers, and gilders also participated in what was intended as an innocent celebration of travel, infused with all the promotional optimism of the Belle Époque.

The kitchens, while not without merit, were never quite a match for this abundant decorative richness. But who really comes to Le Train Bleu for the food? The restaurant was threatened with demolition before being listed as a historic monument in 1972 by André Malraux, then minister of culture. The frescoes were restored and cleaned, to the delight of the prospective passengers.

When the managers of the Café Dôme, René Layon and Ernest Fraux, decided in 1927 to buy a large coal and wood depot opposite their establishment, the proximity of a station—the Gare Montparnasse—was once more a factor. This was no ordinary ambition: the partners aimed to use the 11,000 square feet of space to create the largest brasserie in Paris: La Coupole. But a stronger motivation for such a large-scale project was the effervescence of the Montparnasse area itself. Over the 1920s, Rodin's enigmatic statue of Balzac on carrefour Vavin had watched a huge influx of artists and writers. The Surrealists made it their general headquarters, as did the Lost Generation of the first American exiles in the capital, from Ernest Hemingway and Ezra Pound to Anaïs Nin and Henry Miller. Pretty girls were in plentiful supply as models or muses: Kiki of Montparnasse, Youki Desnos, and Gala Éluard, who ended up with Dalí. The leading lights of avant-garde literature, Aragon, Antonin Artaud, André Breton, Jean Cocteau, and René Daumal, led their own perpetual *grand jeu*, making and breaking friendships with a vengeance. Montparnasse overflowed with energy and ebullience; La Coupole was to galvanize this vitality simply by offering it a space that was big enough to accommodate it.

The premises would effectively be both a brasserie and a café, and would also have a dance-floor in the basement. When it opened, over four hundred staff were employed. The dimensions and the flexibility of La Coupole marked the beginning of a new era. By leaving behind the standard references to Alsace, beer, traveling and railways, the brasserie could become a truly Parisian concept. To support the immense dining area, thirty-two pillars were needed. The proprietors of La Coupole asked local painters to decorate them: some are the work of Fernand Léger, others are by Marie Vassilieff from the Russian Academy in Paris, or Mojzesz Kisling, one of the most prominent representatives of the Parisian School of painting. Today it is difficult to tell which pillar belongs to which artist, but in the absence of any precise attribution, this aspect of the decoration of La Coupole stands as a unique expression of the party spirit that prevailed in Montparnasse at the time. And that spirit has survived: Montparnasse and La Coupole still attract intellectuals and artists. In the 1960s, a clique of young film actors and musicians, among them Pierre Clementi, Jacques Higelin, and Bulle Ogier, formed the "bande de La Coupole," pioneers of the Parisian underground. La Coupole is so much a part of the mythology of Paris that, despite being taken over by Groupe Flo in 1988 and the food being standardized, the place remains a magnet for all those who love space, noise, and a party atmosphere.

LA COUPOLE

There is a Montparnasse variant of Art Deco style, of which La Coupole is the prime example, making this brasserie a sanctuary for the spirit of the 1920s (facing page and above).

Bistros

The Art of Cheap and Cheerful

BARATIN

A table and chair that could be straight out of a Van Gogh painting in this working-class bistro in today's Belleville (preceding page).

AU PETIT RICHE

The entrance and its bar have not changed since 1880, the period when the Petit Riche, the restaurant for the coachmen in the area around the Opéra, became a bourgeois, classier establishment (facing page).

Home cooking has always had its followers in Paris, for reasons of taste as well as economy. Even the most cultivated gastronomes are drawn to the more robust fare served in Paris's *bistrots, bouillons,* and *bistroquets.* Dishes concocted from rustic ingredients, such as the cheaper cuts of beef or a whole range of winter root vegetables—turnips, parsnips, rutabaga—offer the weary palate a substantial connection with the more basic raw materials. These are dishes with density, and, quite literally, bite. Menon, a head cook in the eighteenth century (about whom nothing else seems to be known), published in 1742 a manual of household management for housewives entitled *La Cuisinière Bourgeoise suivie de l'Office, A l'usage de tous ceux qui se mêlent de dépenses de Maisons.* This was the first real treatise on modern household gastronomy, and was updated and reprinted for a century. Bistros began to gain in popularity at the same time as restaurants—indeed they are a proletarian variant of the restaurant (although the customers have never been exclusively poor people; far from it). But they really flourished at the end of the nineteenth century, that overwhelmingly prosperous period for Parisian gastronomy.

The word *bistrot* itself was also coined around this time, and dating its appearance this late can set straight a popular belief about its etymology. Russian Cossacks occupying Paris in 1814 would hasten the innkeepers to serve them at saber-point, to quench their legendary thirst; the received wisdom is that the term was adapted from the Russian word *bystro,* meaning "quickly." Thanks to the work of the linguist Pierre Guiraud, we now know that the word *bistrot* is derived from the word *bistouille,* meaning a bad wine: by association, a bistro would (originally) have been a "place where one drinks bad wine." What is more, the term only started to be used in French to refer to a more upmarket establishment extremely recently, at the end of the 1980s, when home-style cooking came back into fashion.

When it first started in 1854, the Petit Riche near the Opéra was a typical example of the bistro. Haussmann's remodeling of Paris from top to bottom was just getting under way. Little by little, the opera house commissioned by Napoleon III and designed by Charles Garnier started to emerge above this vast building site, the embodiment of the grandeur of the new, wide boulevards. Both high society and the demimonde, politicians, journalists, and actors would crowd into the nearby Café Riche, the Maxim's of the period. But all the little people who formed their invisible escorts—the coachmen, scene-shifters, and theater employees—had nowhere to go and eat. The Petit Riche—an ironic twist on the name of its

AU PETIT RICHE

"Bistro" chairs, brass coat racks, opaline globe lamps, tiled floor: the bourgeois bistro as it was conceived at the beginning of the twentieth century.

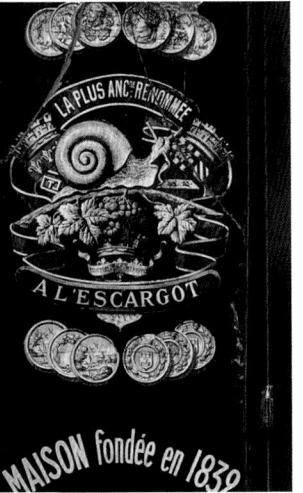  

L'ESCARGOT MONTORGUEIL

The gastropod is everywhere in this bistro on rue Montorgueil in Les Halles: from the reverse-painted glass in the window to the lace curtains (above and facing page). And, of course, on the plates. The spiral staircase of L'Escargot d'Or, the former name of this restaurant, also evokes the proud animal (following double page).

prestigious neighbor—offered them simple but hearty sustenance. The proprietor, a Monsieur Besnard from the Loire Valley, stocked his cellars with Vouvray and Bourgueil, and served typical regional dishes such as crispy pork rillons, green lentil salad, filet de sandre (pikeperch), and géline de Touraine, the local breed of chicken. These are specialties at the Petit Riche to this day.

A fire devastated rue Pelletier in 1873, destroying this unpretentious little restaurant, and paradoxically persuading Monsieur Besnard to make improvements that would turn the Petit Riche into a restaurant aimed at a much classier clientele. The 1880 decor is still visible in the first four dining rooms with their painted-wood ceilings bordered with a frieze of fruits and vegetables in rectangular cartouches, spanned with trompe-l'œil flowers. Large mirrors on the walls are richly engraved with fruit bowls and horns of plenty. The Petit Riche draws in those attending auctions at the nearby Hôtel Drouot, and still retains its hold on some theater people, who have remained faithful to this antiquated but charming place.

L'Escargot Montorgueil is located a stone's throw from the old site of the market at Les Halles. The eating of snails, "which doe ruine to the buddes of vines" as it says in the sixteenth-century almanac *Le Compost des bergers,* has long been a tradition in Paris. The first medieval cookery book, the fourteenth-century *Le Ménagier de Paris* (brought to light in Paris by Jérome Pichon's edition of 1846), gives a vivid recipe where it is recommended to remove the tail: "*et puis leur devez oster leur queue, qui est noire, car c'est leur merde.*" Pliny the Elder advised the consumption of snails for their benefits to the stomach, and all gourmets agree that the sauce is what makes them. The delicacy seems to have reached the height of its popularity in the nineteenth century, a fact borne out by the opening of the specialized establishment L'Escargot Montorgueil in 1875, under a sign proclaiming "Vins, escargots et restaurant." Rue Montorgueil used to be the home of the Paris oyster market, which prompted Jean-Claude Ribaut,

CHARTIER

The decor has not changed at Chartier since 1898: neither the checkered tablecloths, nor the appearance of the waiters. And the clock on the mirror reminds everyone that there is only one hour to eat (above and facing page).

restaurant critic for *Le Monde,* to comment in his *Guide sur les restaurants de Paris* that "the snail is the poor man's oyster." Voltaire even offers an explanation for this in his correspondence, when he praises the aphrodisiac qualities of the little hermaphrodite creature, noting that it is capable "of being in raptures for three or four hours on end."

Before the restaurant, the site had been occupied by L'Escargot d'Or since 1832, simply selling snails and plenty of wine (after all, the persillade sauce served with the snails is well known for making you thirsty). The original frontage in green wood with gilded geometric motifs probably dates from that previous incarnation. But the impressive pediment above the shop front only appeared when the premises were refitted in 1900. The facade is proudly topped by an enormous golden snail, with smaller cast-iron ones at its foot. A glass-fronted panel outside, showing medals won in Paris and Amsterdam, also dates from this renovation, as does the spiral staircase inside, and the glasses engraved with snail shells and horns of plenty full of oysters and crustaceans. In 1919, André Terrail from La Tour d'Argent acquired the business and set about transforming L'Escargot d'Or into a fashionable spot. There were celebrations held after the signing of the Treaty of Versailles, and in 1925 a commemorative painting that had been in Sarah Bernhardt's dining room was mounted on the ceiling. Over the twentieth century, L'Escargot d'Or followed the ups and downs of this quarter of Paris as it was ravaged by idiotic town-planning policies. Today, as Les Halles is on the verge of rebirth, this old place continues to raise its proud horns above the pedestrian street, and be a meeting point for all those who are not frightened off by a cluster of warm snails in garlic sauce.

In 1870, on the eve of the Franco-Prussian War, a butcher named Duval hit upon the idea of the *bouillon,* a working-class restaurant serving only *pot au feu*, the thin beef and vegetable stew that was an economic way for him to use up the poorer cuts of meat. He met with success, and increased the number of outlets, creating a whole chain of *restaurants populaires*—in effect, soup kitchens. Guy de Maupassant's hero in *Bel-Ami,* Georges Duroy, eats there regularly when making his laborious start in journalism, when he has only "six francs fifty left in his pocket." The food was rudimentary, but not devoid of charm, as maintained by the minor dramatist Albert Glatigny in a poem addressed to his contemporary, the food critic Charles Monselet:

> *Tu te voudrais sans doute au fond de tes gargotes*
> *Dans un Bouillon Duval près d'une portion*
> *De lapin contestable ou de bœuf aux carottes...*

Perhaps you would rather be among the greasy spoons

Of a Duval *Bouillon,* tucking into a questionable portion

Of rabbit, or some beef and carrots…

Just off place Clichy, in the unchanged premises now occupied by the Académie de Billard, one of these famous establishments offered quality meals at low prices to all those who needed them, until the 1930s. The Duval formula was quickly imitated, notably by Camille and Édouard Chartier. They stuck to the principle of pot au feu in its broth, but made a selling point out of upgrading the decor. Most of the finer *bouillons* that still exist in Paris, for example the Bouillon Racine in the Latin Quarter, the Bistrot de la Gare in Montparnasse, or Vagenende in Saint-Germain-des-Prés, were either created or bought up by the Chartier brothers. But the *bouillon* on the rue du Faubourg-Montmartre is perhaps their flagship. Opened in 1898, Chartier was aimed at artisans as well as workers, since there were so many in this area. There was clearly a body of very regular customers: after every meal, they would put away their napkins in little numbered wooden compartments. The second room is enormous, and is lit by a glass skylight that covers the entire ceiling. It is divided by two partitions, each marked out with five stout, fixed, coat racks. Mirrors mounted on the walls reflect the animated service. From the wall at the back, a large clock dominates the entire hall, reminding the diners that time is ticking by and they will soon have to go back to work. Over a little more than a century, Chartier prides itself on having served around fifty-five million meals. Today it is as full as it ever was. The high level of noise is compensated by the low level of the prices: most of the main dishes can be had for under ten euros.

The Polidor belongs to a different category of *bouillons* from the end of the nineteenth century, going by the name of *crémerie restaurant.* At first, milk, eggs, and cheese were sold to an early morning clientele, mostly of women, but gradually these businesses changed hands, broadened their outlook, and evolved into delicatessens. Still, for a long time the Polidor kept up a fine reputation for its egg-based dishes. In *Voyage de Sparte* (1883), the nationalist writer Maurice Barrès describes meeting the father of modern phonetics there, Louis Ménard, who recommends to him "the fried egg which one absorbs on the cheap." Jean Paris, in his biography of James Joyce, relates similar peregrinations on the part of the Irish writer, penetrating the Latin Quarter "*à la recherche d'une omelette chez Polidor.*" Generation after generation of penniless writers from the Left Bank were drawn to this unpretentious place. The poet Germain Nouveau, a contemporary of the symbolist Stéphane Mallarmé, celebrates Polidor as a place where "one guzzles magnificently and cheap." Verlaine himself dined there in the company of a Spanish journalist, and Paul Léautaud made it

LE POLIDOR
The dishes are written up on the mirrors with a brush, the frontage bears the word crémerie *in golden letters, and the placemats are paper: Polidor is faithful to the tradition of the family-run bistro (facing page, below, and following double page).*

his regular haunt during the dark times of the Occupation. In 1948, the restaurant became the headquarters of the "Collège de Pataphysique," one of the foundries of experimental postwar literature, involving Raymond Queneau, Eugène Ionesco, Boris Vian, Jacques Prévert, and later, Julio Cortázar. The Collège still holds sessions there. One of the endearing things about Polidor is that, of all the bistros of the last century, it is the one that has best hung onto its original clientele: the real authors of our time are just as fond of it as their illustrious predecessors were. One still receives agreeably brusque treatment from the energetic and mothering waitresses; and one can still, for a few pennies, eat a substantial meal that is not without soul.

ALLARD

Nineteenth-century fare at this bourgeois and comfortable bistro, protected from the ravages of time by its eighteenth-century bars (facing page and above).

In contrast, Allard near place Saint-Michel is a place for powerful editors and powerful men; one of those restaurants where carnal natures seek potent, stimulating food. There are bars on the windows of this authentic eighteenth-century working-class dwelling: a reminder of the prince regent's edict in 1720 requiring wine merchants to safeguard their premises. But the bistro itself only dates from the beginning of the twentieth century. A man from Sancerre by the name of Vincent Candré opened La Halte de l'Éperon on rue de l'Éperon, and the metal sign is still in place today. Candré offered simple wines from his native region and rustic, country-style dishes, concocted by a professional woman chef, "Mère Josephine," one of the first "mères" in Paris. He handed over to a couple from Bourgogne, Marcel and Marthe Allard, who continued the custom introduced by the cook of a thoroughly regular menu: Monday, Toulouse cassoulet; Tuesday, veal à la berrichonne; Wednesday, navarin of lamb; Thursday, petit salé with lentils; Friday, braised beef and carrots; Saturday, coq au vin. The star dish for special occasions was duck with olives. This sequence is still available on the menu, or rather on the tables, since there are no individual portions at Allard: the casserole dish or terrine is placed directly on the tablecloth and everyone takes what they want. Ever since the restaurant was founded, the public entrance has been via the kitchen, which really

L'AMI LOUIS

The stove (facing page) inevitably evokes the wartime period, as do the checkered curtains in the front window (one almost expects Jean Gabin to pop out from behind them). Walls and ceilings are never repainted; simply revarnished on top of the layers of smoke. The typically Parisian vaulted cellars hold some memorable bottles (above).

epitomizes the spirit of the place. You come here to tie your napkin around your neck, and solemnly dig in to large amounts of substantial, filling food.

The little bistro L'Ami Louis has been tucked away behind the place de la République and the large boulevards since 1934, but it only really took off after World War II. Due to historical happenstance, and its own particular charm, it has become known as a rendezvous for Americans in Paris. The decor, it has to be said, does seems to be straight out of *An American in Paris* or *Gigi*. Baskets of fruit and vegetables are laid out at the back like in a market; the look is so quintessentially "French bistro" that it matches the Hollywood ideal of the capital. It is hardly surprising then that a club of American billionaires fly over every year in their jets for a private dinner in the restaurant. Bill Clinton and Jacques Chirac set the example in July 1999.

In fact, L'Ami Louis has been a landmark for Americans since 1944, when intelligence officers in the OSS—including Jack Warner, the youngest of the Warner Brothers—set up their headquarters there. Americans have remained loyal, and the place has become synonymous, in the United States, with the small Parisian bistro, picturesque and not too expensive. While the dollar was strong, that is: in local terms, the prices (like the portions) can reach Himalayan dimensions. You come here for the simple potluck style of the place, the gigantic ribs of beef and the mountains of matchstick potatoes, but you can expect to blow the limit on your American Express. It has become a trendy spot for the Parisian showbiz set as well. It suits the solid appetites of "outdoor writers" too: you might find Jim Harrison here after signing a profitable contract. All in all, L'Ami Louis is pure Hollywood, right down to the bill. Such is the price of success for this most American of Parisian bistros.

Since the 1980s, the bistro has made a strong comeback in Paris. A new generation of chefs left the big hotels and headed instead for the kitchens of minor sites on their periphery, where they could prove themselves. Yves Camdeborde was the first: he had been at Le Crillon when he opened the Régalade, near

the Porte d'Orléans. His southwestern influences from Béarn and the Basque Country quickly drew in lovers of traditional charcuterie, piperade with fried Bayonne ham, and hachis Parmentier with boudin noir black sausage. Thierry Breton on the other hand, at Chez Michel behind the Gare du Nord, is dedicated to the flavors of the west. Thierry Faucher at L'Os à Mœlle in the distant fifteenth arrondissement, offers a simple table d'hôte where the blanquette has become legendary; Rodolphe Paquin is at Repaire de Cartouche, between Bastille and Nation, a Norman inn in the middle of bohemian Paris, where they serve freshly farm-killed pork. They have all adopted the same model: economical products, but good quality, prepared with all the attention to detail of high gastronomic style, coupled with cleverly selected wines from lesser-known regions. And the bill is as light as the preparations.

The emergence of these unconventional bistros made the Parisian gourmet scene suddenly much more lively. The Michelin-starred restaurateur Michel Rostang set the tone by developing his concept of *bistrots d'à côté,* or "next-door" bistros: he is now onto his third, in the west of Paris. Rostang's chefs train in his eponymous flagship restaurant, absorbing a generous style tinged with bourgeois manners. His interiors are brightened up by collections of old editions of the *Michelin Guide*, Parisian slipware figures, and antique stoves; reconditioned sites that are as successful as ever.

    Alain Ducasse took over an old bistro in the centre of Paris in the year 2000, Aux Lyonnais, the once-favorite haunt for coachmen killing time waiting for shows to finish at the Opéra-Comique. He spruced up the decor, which is based around the same tilework as the Paris Metro, and rejuvenated the cuisine. The result is a Parisian version of a Lyon *bouchon* or tavern. The pike quenelles are probably the lightest in Paris. This year, he extended his empire by taking over Benoît, a luxury bistro situated near the Hôtel de Ville, which has been part of the routine of city councillors since 1912.

AUX LYONNAIS

Alain Ducasse has brought this Lyon-style mâchon *back to its former glory. The ceramic tiles are the same as those in the Paris Metro (facing page and above). The mahogany bar has not changed since the coachmen used to come and lean on it (following double page).*

In fact a turn towards a more domestic style of cooking has been seen right across the range of Parisian gastronomy, including the most upmarket tables. Here is Albert Glatigny again:

Eh bien, oui ! j'aime un plat canaille
Bien mieux que ces combinaisons
Qu'un chef alambique et travaille...

Well, yes I do like a no-frills dish
Much better than these combinations
Made so much of by a chef...

Women chefs were not far behind in becoming stars of the stoves again. Hélène Darroze, with her two stars in the *Michelin Guide*, got her hands on a very trendy place in the sixth arrondissement, where the substantial dishes of her native southwest are not neglected. The daughters of great chefs have been getting down to it as well. Sophie Bardet, at Point Bar (guided by her old man, the great cook from Touraine, Jean Bardet), and Caroline Rostang at L'Absinthe, have engaged in friendly culinary combat on the place du Marché-Saint-Honoré. And Paris can be proud to continue the historic "mère" tradition of women chefs, after the Joséphines, Fernandes, and Adriennes of the past. Raquel Carena arrived from Argentina as a teenager. In 1987, she walked into a bistro in the multicultural Belleville area of Paris and took over a minuscule galley kitchen, from where she would conquer the city. Assisted out front by Philippe Pinoteau, she gave center stage to her ingredients, preparing them with a simplicity that won over the most blasé palates. Her vegetables come from the best truck farmer supplying Paris, Joël Thiébault, and her meats from the cult butcher of the fifth arrondissement, Jean Marie Charcellay. The fish comes from the dockside market in Le Guilvinec in Brittany. Nice little table wines from great winemakers and coffee from Café Verlet round off a very astute and very tasty experience. An evening at Le Baratin is a dive into authentic Paris, where you sit elbow-to-elbow with writers, pretty girls, and local inhabitants, including the great photographer Willy Ronis (the walls bear a number of his prints of Paris, given by him in appreciation). The kitchen door is always open, and Raquel Carena looks out over the dining area, a little like an actor watching the reactions of the audience through a hole in the curtain. There is no menu: the dishes change every day depending on what the market inspires, and are written up on a black slate. Raquel Carena is the best embodiment of domestic-style *cuisine ménagère* in Paris today. Her bistro is always full: proof that the Parisians have not lost their taste for simple pleasures.

LE BARATIN
The ceremonious display of the wine list and, vitally, the plats du jour, on a blackboard, is synonymous with the culture of the contemporary bistro (facing page). Raquel Carena, the owner-chef of this high-class tavern, writes them up herself, depending on the seasonal and daily availability of her ingredients (above).

LE BARATIN
The walls of Le Baratin are hung with works by local artists from Belleville, which still has a village feel. The photographer Willy Ronis (back wall) often comes here as a neighbor and friend.

Contemporary Settings

The Future Perfect

Then came nouvelle cuisine. And with it, the whole question of the relationship between the creative act that is gastronomy, and contemporary art. The young chefs of the 1960s who wanted to find a space for themselves that broke with tradition were thinking in exactly the same avant-garde way as contemporary artists. Presentation on the plate is an aesthetic matter requiring careful thought; references were sought and found in abstract painting. From there, it was a small step to extend these considerations to the objects surrounding the plate, and the wider setting within which the ceremony of a gastronomic meal takes place. A number of chefs of this generation have continued to collaborate with famous artists and interior designers to create a coherent environment. In 2000, Guy Savoy asked Jean-Michel Wilmotte (who had redesigned the street furniture on the Champs-Élysées) to invent a new interior for his restaurant on rue Troyon. In 2003, Alain Dutournier commissioned the Argentinian painter Alberto Bali to work on his Carré des Feuillants. In both cases, the use of contemporary works and primitive pieces highlights the common ground between the intentionally innovative gastronomic offering, and the abstract forms so characteristic of modern art. This trend was started in Paris by a great chef who is rather less talked about today, Claude Peyrot. His restaurant Le Vivarois opened in 1966 on avenue Victor-Hugo in the sixteenth arrondissement. It was wall-to-wall Knoll International: Saarinen chairs, with walls covered in beige silk and peppered with framed prints. The design provoked sarcastic comments at the time, and subsequently was paradoxically criticized for being "dated." It would probably be back in fashion now, as would Peyrot's cuisine, with its warm oysters and curry, snails with a leek persillade, and chocolate tarte fondante.

Slightly later examples of this style, characterized by refined elegance without ostentation, are still to be found in Paris. The Flora Danica and the Copenhague, the two restaurants owned by the Danish cultural center, the Maison du Danemark, in the Champs-Élysées, were first opened in 1955. When they were completely redecorated in 1973, the work followed strict Scandinavian creative criteria, and included the famous purple eggshell-shaped armchairs by Arne Jacobsen. Though refurbished in 2002, the decor in both restaurants remains distinctly 1970s. In Flora Danica the tables and chairs are in light wood, and the fixed bench seats and cardboard lampshades are orange. The Copenhague has very contemporary armchairs in bright red leather, set around strictly white tables. The uncluttered decor harmonizes with precepts of Scandinavian cuisine.

CAFÉ BEAUBOURG

With its exposed concrete columns, polished concrete floor, and functional walkways and furniture, this café-restaurant designed by Christian de Portzamparc for the Costes brothers at the beginning of the 1980s remains one of the most significant creations of the talented partnership.

GUY SAVOY

Jean-Michel Wilmotte's design for Guy Savoy's flagship restaurant puts the accent on noble materials and primitive art. Here in the smaller dining area, a partition in wenge wood and an African sculpture (facing page).

To understand what a clean break the designs of Le Vivarois and the Danish restaurants represented, one has to place oneself in the historical context. A particular sort of restaurant had flourished during the 1950s, a sort of neo-roadside-inn to be found up and down the country as well as in Paris. The walls would be lined with rows of copper saucepans and hunting trophies, the chairs were upright Louis XIII style, upholstered in Genoa velvet, and the tables were solid oak. These establishments, dripping in "early Merovingian" historicism, perpetuated the myth of a rural France that was fast disappearing. This was a period when food critics with questionable political pasts would intone reverently about country cooking, *à la* Curnonsky, the famous French gastronome whose favored cooking style, rich in sauces and flavors, had dominated restaurants of the interwar period. The whole country was engaged in a backward-looking fervor in which coq au vin, crêpes suzette, and quenelle de brochet were glorified in a Lewis Carroll-style jumbled celebration. The serving staff still played a vital role in the ceremony of a restaurant meal: carving and flambéing at a side table were de rigueur, as were the convoys of cheese and dessert trolleys. As a result, the restaurant manager or head waiter normally held a much more prominent position than the chef. Then the shock of nouvelle cuisine came and wiped all this solemn formality away. Chefs were allowed space to develop in the foreground. Plates would arrive as finished presentations, rather than being constructed at the table. The physical theater of the waiter metamorphosed into a more serious dramatic style, where manual dexterity was less important than a smooth patter to sell you the chef's culinary breakthroughs and distract you from the price of the wine. Some great Parisian restaurants have stuck to the old tradition. La Tour d'Argent of course, but Lasserre even more so, where the surprisingly eclectic decor embodies both the personality of its illustrious founder, Roger Lasserre, and the spirit of those quiet times in the 1950s when pleasantness and luxurious comfort were more important than stylistic coherence.

Whereas the staunch would-be classicism of the 1950s ended up becoming slightly pompous, the two following decades in Paris were marked by a cheerful recycling of styles, as if the city intended to use its restaurant interiors to flaunt its own historical diversity. One name embodies this enthusiastic (if not entirely rigorous) hodgepodge, more than any other: the iconoclastic Bill Slavik. He first stood out for his surrealist staging of the Drugstore Saint-Germain, on the corner of the boulevard Saint-Germain and rue de Rennes, which is now occupied by an Armani shop. Parisians remember this place as revolutionary in its time, where you could get something to eat until two in the morning, and buy records, newspapers, books, and cigarettes. On the awnings, Slavik had put casts of the hands and lips of film stars, loaded with an erotic charge that bewitched the imagination of the young people hanging around there looking for adventure.

Details from Philippe Starck's resolutely eclectic interior, perhaps a modern take on the Napoleon III style of the mid-nineteenth century, with its button-tufted walls, stuffed rhinoceros head, mock African art, and designer armchairs and tables (preceding pages).

LE JULES VERNE
Slavik's scheme for this exceptional location opens vistas onto the Parisian landscape, yet carefully preserves the intimacy of the diners (facing page).

Slavik next took on the bistro style, and delivered a baroque version of it at the brasserie Muniche on rue de Buci. This site has also disappeared, but many echoes of it remain, in L'Européen opposite the Gare de Lyon, or at the Petit Mâchon on rue de la Convention. Slavik became *the* restaurant designer in Paris at the end of the 1960s, trotting out variations on ultra-kitsch settings ad nauseam. But before bowing out, he performed one final metamorphosis in 1983: the Jules Verne. This was to be situated halfway up the Eiffel Tower, on a specially built platform above the second level, amid the wheels and pulleys of the elevator machinery. Slavik's design for this mechanical and aerial microcosm—halfway between city and sky; made of stone and steel—is based on a Jules Verne theme, and evokes the huge vessels in his literature: the *Albatross* in *Robur the Conqueror* or Captain Nemo's *Nautilus*. The low ceiling and discreet lancet windows on the facade give the restaurant a paradoxical intimacy. The space is arranged in a petal structure, offering tempting access to three views. The bar looks out onto the Champ-de-Mars and Les Invalides, the main dining area overlooks Notre Dame and the historic center of Paris, and the second dining area looks out at the Palais de Chaillot and on to La Défense. Slavik willingly abandoned his flamboyant style to leave these impressive panoramas alone, and not distract the guest from some of the finest views in the world. By doing this, he achieved his cleanest and most successful design. He chose to blend with the colors and materials of the tower, using a monochrome matt gray that eliminates glare and reflections. The lattice of gloss black perforated-steel tiles on the ceiling echoes the geometric framework of the tower. The black and gray speckled carpet, the pepper-and-salt wooden tables with black bases, covered with gray glazed linen cloths, the "office" chairs in cast iron covered with a mottled, shagreen-like leatherette, the steel bar and the shiny piano facing it create an ensemble of precision and elegance.

The standard of the food had to be high, to match the towering setting. Alain Reix, formerly of Le Divellec, one of the best fish restaurants in Paris, has been at the helm of this remarkable establishment since 1992. His menu is both generous and precise, and is characterized by daring combinations of flavors, compensated by a sense of culinary balance. Lobster accompanied by caramelized tomato and fennel; turbot with a celery and green-mango garnish and kaffir-lime sauce; these are dishes that take the taste buds on a journey just as Jules Verne took his readers, without risk or danger, but to the greatest pleasure of the diners.

With Slavik, the role of interior designer reached star status. But the corresponding function of commissioning the work is of course just as important; we sometimes forget that the Renaissance owed as much to Lorenzo de Medici as Leonardo da Vinci. Two brothers from Aveyron in the south of France, Gilbert and Jean-Louis Costes, were to bring an equivalent kudos to this role. At the beginning of the 1980s, the Costes brothers started to change from small-time café owners into patrons of the arts; they decisively launched artists, architects, and interior designers into restaurant work, nurturing talent that would go on to define the two following decades. Some of the names alone indicate the influence of their patronage: Philippe Starck, Christian de Portzamparc, and Jacques Garcia. Starck was an unknown

when Jean-Louis Costes asked him to design the interior of Café Costes in 1983. Portzamparc had won the competition for the Cité de la Musique at La Villette, but his reputation had not extended beyond a specialist inner circle when he was given the contract for the Café Beaubourg in 1986. Jacques Garcia was well known to the rich private clients whose interiors he worked on, but his contribution to Hôtel Costes in 1996 signaled the emergence of a neo-Rococo style, which projected the global supremacy of Parisian gastronomy via the art of interior design. The developer as patron made a fundamental contribution in each case, requiring not only complicity of taste with the artist, but more importantly, a fully professional conception of the evolving restaurant, predating the artist's involvement.

The Hôtel Costes is probably their most significant contribution to the revival of the Parisian restaurant scene. A network of rooms is arranged around a patio with ocher-painted facades, like a Roman villa; the decoration vaguely borrows from a Napoleon III theme, reworked by the eclectic mind of Jacques Garcia. The result is a labyrinthine place that has become one of the secret centers of today's Parisian elite.

It is interesting to compare this interior with that of Le Bélier on rue de Beaux-Arts, which was also created by Jacques Garcia, in the 1990s. It is a simpler space, naturally lit from a veranda and a small courtyard with a fountain, and by an overhead opening veiled by an ivory canvas awning. At night the light comes from old copper lanterns suspended from the ceiling. The inspiration is Empire style: upright armchairs, chaise-longues, carpets with scrolling foliage, drapery, and those columns he likes so much. There is a pervading atmosphere of gold and green, in keeping with the spirit of the chosen period. How is it then that this design, in all its profusion, is less than convincing? The restaurant owner, rather than

LE BÉLIER

Jacques Garcia is all about dramatizing an atmosphere, with drapes, silk-lined walls, sconces, added marble columns, and a whole series of design accessories that together give the impression of always having been there, as shown here in the restaurant of the Hôtel des Beaux-Arts (facing page and above).

LE BÉLIER

*Jacques Garcia works like
a cinematographer, developing
illusions to give an impression
of reality.*

trying to manipulate the traditional restaurant space, has relinquished it to the sumptuous and kitsch devices of the designer. What we have here is unfortunately a rather ordinary dining room, which feels stuck on, rather than truly inspired. The food at this privately owned hotel betrays the same lack of decisiveness: it hesitates between a fairly classic menu (sole meunière, slow-cooked lamb shanks, veal kidney fricassée, chocolate moelleux, etc.) and offerings that border on room-service food (club sandwich, plate of seasonal vegetables). Which all goes to show that it takes more than a great name in interior design, however inspired he might be, to give a gastronomic identity to a restaurant, and all the more so for a hotel restaurant.

The same could not be said about Bernard Pacaud's L'Ambroisie, a restaurant that truly breathes a spirit of authenticity, despite being a complete reconstruction. Here there is a perfect balance between cuisine and decor: the former, perfectionist and untouchable in its classicism; the latter, seemingly straight out of a private mansion in the Marais. The same meticulousness that governs Bernard Pacaud's culinary artistry—he is the spiritual heir of the famous Mère Brazier—is to be found in the details of the furniture and fittings. Some are accumulated antiques, some elements are reconstructions by François-Joseph Graf. Nothing is from one period, yet everything is authentic; the trompe-l'œil succeeds perfectly. The stucco cornices supported by their marble consoles, the chandeliers, and the gold-leaf mirrors all seem to have been there for ever. This is an illusion: everything in this part of the building on place des Vosges has been remodeled, starting with the volume of the three rooms, which had the floors lowered and the ceilings raised. In a major piece of work, François-Joseph Graf has managed to bring harmony to a heterogeneous

L'AMBROISIE

Bernard Pacaud's famous restaurant on place des Vosges gives the illusion of coming straight out of the seventeenth century. François-Joseph Graf, with exquisite attention to the smallest details, has created the perfect trompe-l'œil, combining authentic elements—the Beauvais tapestries or the Köln chairs from the Vienna Opera—with expertly reconstituted features (facing page, above, and following double page).

**L'ATELIER DE
JOËL ROBUCHON**

*The culinary space of the Hôtel
Pont-Royal has something
of a contemporary museum
feeling (facing page and below).
Ingredients and finished dishes
alike seem to be behind glass,
although the proximity of guests
to the kitchen is supposed to
abolish this distance. Elsewhere,
shared tables look out onto the
street, keeping the bar-top
concept Robuchon likes
(following pages).*

ensemble of elements. So even if the Köln chairs from the Vienna Opera are typical of 1900, and the Beauvais tapestries on the wall date from the end of the Enlightenment, and the French crystal chandeliers hanging from the ceiling exude an essence of the seventeenth-century, L'Ambroisie is bathed in a sort of sovereign timelessness that places it beyond, and even above, specific fashions. The same is true of Bernard Pacaud's deceptively simple preparations. Pacaud is heir to a modest but vital tradition in great French cookery, whose gastronomy stayed as close to its ingredients as possible. This leading chef shows perfect technique and faultless integrity: no show-off dishes, just flawless interpretation of the great gastronomic classics, in keeping with a place that glows with a patina of good taste.

We have seen how the restaurant chef gradually gained control and supplanted the maitre d'. Sooner or later, this change in the balance of power was bound to show in the architecture of restaurants themselves. Joël Robuchon, one of the best-known international restaurateurs, deliberately and very publicly went into retirement at the turn of the millennium. Then in 2003 he returned to the restaurant scene with a new concept: the open kitchen, immediately arousing lively controversy. But the idea caught the imagination of the Parisian public, who were, at least to begin with, charmed by the prospect of a gastronomic snack-bar, L'Atelier de Joël Robuchon. At Robuchon's request, designer Pierre-Yves Rochon placed thirty-eight stools backed in red leather around a rosewood bar looking directly onto the assembly area of the kitchen. The kitchen staff, all dressed in the same colors, busy themselves before your eyes. Spanish hams stand ready on their *jamoneros;* glass bowls filled with blocks of ice are imperiously topped by pyramids of langoustine; glass and steel shelves show bottle-ends off to good effect. The staging aims to be sober yet functional, reflecting a style of cooking that makes many references to the Japanese art of food preparation and presentation. There is an imposed economy of taste that borders on self-denial;

a "this is the way things are" attitude that aims to break the culinary ritual out of its supposedly starchy formality. Yet a human element has been removed: the service is made *less* personal and one feels a distance where there could be human contact with a maitre d', or wine waiter. As those in the line outdoors envy each occupied stool and wait for one to be free, those indoors remain on the outside of an experience which, after all, is not very participative. The open kitchen cannot rid itself of an aquarium feel, and the absence of any intermediary has a disorienting effect. The result is proof that a desire to "open out" is not enough: communication is also essential, of emotions, or at least aromas and voices, which, in this strange, insulated place, seem peculiarly stifled.

PINXO

Just near rue Saint-Honoré, Pinxo draws you in to a friendly shared experience with its dishes à partager *(above), closely spaced tables (facing page), and plating kitchen open to the dining area (following pages).*

Curiously enough, with a similar concept and the same designer, Alain Dutournier's Pinxo at the Plaza Paris Vendôme hotel manages to be a perfectly convivial place. Presumably this is because the restaurateur gives proper emphasis to human contact. Visual access to the kitchen is reserved here for a dozen aficionados at a black granite bar, who follow the final phase of the preparation of dishes with interest, the kitchen as such being situated in the basement. The rest of the diners occupy the main room, which is bathed in natural light. Beige blinds filter the light from outside to soothing effect. The materials used are simple: wood and granite for the tables, black leather for the chairs, whitewashed walls. This discreet and elegant design does not get between the guest and the food, which combines playful fusion with a respect for country produce. Inspired by the culture of Spanish tapas—*pintxos* in Basque—Alain Dutournier has instituted a "sharing" concept: each dish is served in mini-portions so that everybody around the table can dip in as they wish and enjoy the meal in its entirety. From chilled piperade, poached eggs, and pan-fried shavings of matured ham, to tataki of salmon, or Granny Smith apple with horseradish and sweet and sour ginger, the menu proposes a respectful journey among the flavors of the ingredients, without anything jerky or aggressive. Pinxo is a civilized place, built around contemporary fashion, but most importantly it favors the ideas of pleasure and comfort. The public in this area—the highly trendy Saint-Honoré district—know a good thing when they see one, and they have chosen Pinxo as their regular canteen, which is a much more difficult distinction to obtain than a star in the *Michelin Guide*. The talented Dutournier has caught the attention of the fickle world of Parisian fashion, and has managed to get them in, keep them in, and keep them coming back.

The same regard for conviviality is evident at Le Chiberta, an old Parisian establishment just off the Champs-Élysées, taken over by Guy Savoy in August 2004. The interior was redesigned by Jean-Michel Wilmotte along resolutely contemporary lines. The leading architect's objective was to have different categories of diners come together in a relatively homogeneous space: businesspeople negotiating a contract, couples dining tête-à-tête, families or groups of friends gathered around a good meal. In Guy Savoy's mind, the one common element to these different worlds is wine, because of its implication of sharing, and he wanted it to be brought into the foreground. Wilmotte obliged with a *cave de jour* where you can see the bottles arranged horizontally behind temperature-controlled glass,

sporting their multicolored labels. This functional design is visible from the entrance area, and is repeated in the secluded dining room where it takes up an entire wall. At the other end of the restaurant, socializing is encouraged at a square bar with about twenty places; cleaved slate blocks surround the top edge and proffer a surface of off-white Corian, a high-tech material combining natural minerals and pure acrylic polymers. One can sit at the bar and grab a bite in a table d'hôte atmosphere, which is once again becoming more fashionable in Paris. A few artworks punctuate the black walls: a digital reproduction on canvas of a detail from a street scene by Bertrand Lavier, and three large, colored flats with shimmering back tones by Gérard Traquandi, which are both abstract and sensual.

LE CHIBERTA
Wine is omnipresent at Le Chiberta, bringing warmth to Jean-Michel Wilmotte's dimly lit, meeting-friendly interior (facing page and above).

Guy Savoy's generous cuisine aims first of all to promote the intrinsic quality of the products he gets from his suppliers, among the best in France. The associations he makes are never fussy; they are limited to two or three flavors, combined in such a way that each enhances the other. Roasted langoustine with herb fritters is a harmony of sea and garden; the smooth texture of barely seared tuna is led by a rocket-oil dressing into the contrasting crunch of grilled beans. Another example is the alliance of roast, braised, or pan-fried meats with fruits and condiments: braised veal shank with peaches, pigeon and Espelette pepper, or shoulder of lamb and lemon confit. In only a year, this place has become an essential address on the gourmet map, combining as it does a youthful attitude to gastronomy, a respect for produce, and a relaxing environment: a real contrast with the constrained ceremony of the grand, traditional French restaurant.

LE CHIBERTA
*Another way of enjoying
a meal: eating around
the bar, elbow-to-elbow
with other guests.*

L'ALCAZAR

At L'Alcazar, behind Saint-Germain-des-Prés, there is always somewhere to look: into the kitchens, up to the mezzanine or down onto the open and spacious main room, an authentic latter-day brasserie (facing page and above). The bar on the mezzanine has fat cushions, bluish lighting overhead, and chairs that are very Conran Shop. The salt and pepper holders, ashtray, and vase were, of course, designed by the English master (following pages).

A breeze from across the Channel has brought success to L'Alcazar, the contemporary brasserie created by Sir Terence Conran in 1998. This followed his success with Bluebird, which opened in London the previous year, but Terence Conran has been in love with continental food culture for a long time. As an unknown designer in 1953 he opened the Soup Kitchen in London, which bore the distinction of being the first place in the capital to offer decent espresso. Many restaurants followed in Great Britain, but also in New York, Stockholm, and, of course, Paris. Over thirty restaurants all over the world now operate under the banner of Conran Restaurants. L'Alcazar, just near the École des Beaux-Arts and Saint-Germain-des-Prés, was originally a court where *le jeu de paume,* the French precursor of tennis, was played. Then it was a printer's, then the home of Jean-Marie Rivière's orchestral cabaret. The large, airy space, lit by a glass roof, was ideal for the creation of a sort of loft on two floors, with the restaurant dining area on the ground floor and a trendy bar above. Eight red columns structure the large lower room, which is glazed on one side to allow diners to watch the activity in the kitchens. Bench seats in burgundy velvet occupy the centre of the atrium, while the wall opposite the kitchen has angled mirrors above the tables, encouraging sneaky glances at surrounding tables.

Upstairs, the bar is arranged as a mezzanine around the room below, offering views of the restaurant from all angles. Fun cushions are scattered on the seats, providing patches of pure color here and there, and stylized low armchairs in white wicker reinforce the impression of being in a children's playground. And since the guests are forced to talk louder and higher than the delightfully bracing techno music, this impression tends to get stronger throughout the evening. L'Alcazar is clearly a Parisian prototype of the trendy hangout, and Sir Terence Conran has hit on a formula that

successfully draws a young crowd into his restaurant. The food has simple and unsophisticated aims, in line with the tastes of an age range that is not quite out of its gastronomic childhood: seafood platters, fish and chips for a bit of London color, and a whole variety of basic country dishes, from boudin noir with chestnuts and apple, to Landes farm chicken stuffed with foie gras, grenaille potatoes with a jus, and shoulder of lamb confit with thyme.

Near to the Italianate arches on rue de Rivoli can be found the work of a Parisian designer with strong influences from Ettore Sottsass in Milan. Olivier Gagnère has given a neoclassical slant to the historic Marly wing of the Louvre. The site, obtained by the Costes brothers in 1994, overlooks the Ieoh Ming Pei pyramid, posing delicate problems of integration for a café-restaurant. Olivier Gagnère is used to working with traditional luxury artisans, such as Murano Glassware and Bernardaud Porcelaine. He responded elegantly to the challenge of Le Café Marly, without renouncing any of his sense of new lines. The furniture and lighting schemes fit well into three rooms painted in warm colors: burgundy red for the large one, and cashmere gray for the two little annexes that look onto rue de Rivoli. At the centre of each inner wall, Gagnère has traced a square in gold leaf, a stylized reminder of the period when the nobility of France filled these halls. Although the chairs are modern, their shape echoes Empire furniture, and each one bears a gold ring on its back, the designer's signature mark. On the ceiling is an admirable crystal chandelier designed by Gagnère and made by Murano in Venice, which stretches out and unfurls like the snake Moses threw at Pharaoh's feet. Other lamps in black metal stand on the ground like totems, with a vaguely African air about them. The diners in this unusual place are a curious mixture of regulars, slightly lost-looking tourists, art-lovers, young women pausing for a breather from shopping, and businessmen relaxing off the clock. Le Café Marly lends itself to long meditations after lunch, or idle afternoon trysts spent tackling the meaning of life. A reasonable and basic menu in the contemporary bistro spirit of the Costes brothers completes this welcome halt in the great urban confusion that surrounds it.

One step further beyond the real world takes us into the new Maison Baccarat on the place des États-Unis, the former residence of Marie-Laure de Noailles, the muse of Jean Cocteau, Salvador Dalí, Luis Buñuel, and Man Ray. From the 1920s to the 1950s this Haussmann mansion hosted some of the most surreal parties in Paris, from the Bal des Matières in 1929 to the Bal de la Lune sur Mer in 1951, before the doors closed on this epoch of hyper-creativity (never to reopen, unfortunately). But the famous crystal

LE CAFÉ MARLY
The terrace of Le Café Marly looks onto the Louvre pyramid (facing page). Tourists and all sorts of Parisians relax there in the summer months, while the three rooms inside, dressed by Olivier Gagnère, look as if they belong in a very elitist club (below). The chairs with brass rings and feet and the Murano chandelier are signature elements of Gagnère's design (following double page).

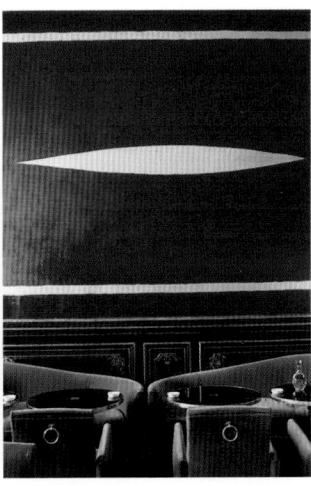

manufacturing firm Baccarat, in choosing this building in 2003 to house their management offices and museum, saw an opportunity to prove themselves equal to the place and its legend. The architect in charge of recreating the interior was Philippe Starck, well known for his whimsical and expressionistic style, and for revolutionizing all the objects and spaces he touches (and he touches everything). Starck—also discovered by the Costes brothers—designed the first modern café in Paris at the end of the 1970s, Café Costes, which today has disappeared. There, he did away with the archetypal leatherette and vinyl decor, and replaced it with raw materials and a rock 'n' roll atmosphere. Since then he has been transforming atmospheres all over the world, from

Hong Kong to Mexico, via London and Miami, with an acute sense of personal metamorphosis, whether it be in hotels, restaurants, or showrooms. Not to mention the innumerable everyday objects, furniture, and household appliances whose shapes he has remodeled.

**CRISTAL ROOM
DE BACCARAT**
Walls stripped back to the brick and a profusion of crystal: Philippe Starck plays brutally with contrasts in this fantastical palace, seemingly dreamed up rather than designed, transforming the former private residence of Marie-Laure de Noailles (facing page and above).

It is clear, even from the outside of this private building near the place de l'Étoile, that Starck has made Baccarat into a baroque fairyland. Crystal is of course the favored material, and its juxtaposition with white stone reveals secret hues within, hidden until now. The severe Parisian classicism is thus suddenly rejuvenated, as if a once polychromatic Gothic cathedral were restored in all its color. The monumental hall contains a chandelier held by a hand, mounted on a large mirror, and drapes supported by fine crystal columns: a reference to the the castle in Cocteau's film of *Beauty and the Beast*. On either side of the entrance, two Baccarat vases that belonged to the emperor of Ethiopia miraculously start to talk. A projection makes two faces appear on their fusible surface, like Gorgon's heads bathed in a milky substance, and they deliver measured words about the crystal makers' ancestral craft. On the ground, an illuminated carpet indicates the mysterious path to follow. At the foot of the stairs, a candelabra made for Tsar Nicolas II looks over an enormous chair and a footstool to match, threatening to send the visitor who dares to confront them back to the world of Alice in Wonderland. As you climb the stairs to the Cristal Room restaurant, a chandelier with 157 lights turns slowly above your head. You eventually enter the large salon. In a space dedicated to transparency, Philippe Starck has had the inspired idea of stripping sections of wall completely, contrasting the bare original brick with the brilliance of the crystal, the silkiness of the sofas, and the metallic reflections of the furniture. Four large pink-and-white cameos of

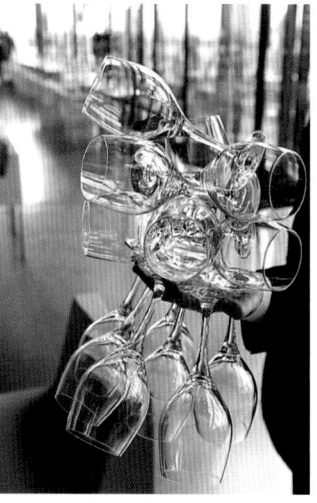

GEORGES

The restaurant of the Centre Georges Pompidou is a contemporary art installation, playing on the themes of inside and outside, organic and metallic, transparent and opaque. Another attractive feature of Georges is its fabulous terrace overhanging the zinc roofs of old Paris (above, facing, and following pages).

Louis XIV and members of his court frame the room. Parisians obviously come here for the decor: it is a feast for the eyes. But thanks to the chef, Thierry Burlot, it is a feast for the taste buds, too. Burlot produces seasonal cuisine that promotes the quality of the ingredients, and offers a wine list with *grands crus* to do justice to the majesty of this Grand Siècle dining room.

Thierry Costes, the son of Gilbert Costes, has followed in the family footsteps of breathing new life into the restaurant business. For Georges, the restaurant on the sixth floor of the Centre Georges Pompidou, he called on two young talents of contemporary architecture, the Frenchman Dominique Jakob and the New Zealander Brendan MacFarlane, to work in conjunction with the agency Archilab. Into the measured dimensions of Richard Rogers and Renzo Piano's cubic structure—which is left untouched down to the smallest aeration duct—they have introduced opaque aluminum "volumes" colored red, yellow, and blue. A new space is defined by these forms, which seem to emerge from the ground like outgrowths, spreading out in lava floes like the sculptor César's foam *Expansions*. This opposition of organic forms with the glass and steel structure of the museum is echoed by the presence on each table of a single rose, raising its head with fragile pride above the steel tables and white leather chairs; a virtual garden that strikes the eye when you enter each area. Jakob and MacFarlane started their career with private commissions, notably the acclaimed Maison T in La Garenne-Colombes to the northwest of Paris, where their capacity to adopt organic forms was already in evidence. More recently, they have been chosen to fit out Magasins Réunis, an industrial structure next to the Seine in the thirteenth arrondissement, as

part of a waterfront regeneration scheme along the lines of London's Docklands. Georges has very quickly become one of the trendiest tables in the capital, a mix of showbiz people, movie people, and contemporary art people with their groupies, models and fashion designers, all mixed with tourists attracted by the exceptional view the restaurant offers over Paris. Inevitably, arguments arise over seating, with the strategic spots near the picture windows, or the red "volume" for VIPs, being the most sought-after. The waiting staff (composed principally of young women with interminable legs and catalog smiles) struggle to arbitrate over these disputes. The cuisine rides the crest of an overtly fusion wave—prawn ravioli with hoisin sauce, Peking duck with caramel, tuna or salmon tartar—before gliding in to a "diet" version of chocolate fondant, invented by Michel Bras and now cropping up in all the fashionable restaurants. It should be noted however that Georges is the only place in Paris where one can find Pacific "Black Cod," as fatty and melt-in-the-mouth as you could wish. For that, Paris's true gastronomes also go to Georges, and they don't care where they sit.

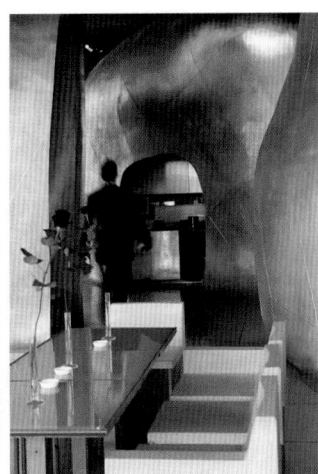

GEORGES
An avenue of roses under the mouth of a volcano? An airport lounge? A funeral parlor? Panoramic viewpoint, or entrance to the catacombs? Georges offers all these possibilities, a work open to a multitude of interpretations (facing page and above).

LE SQUARE TROUSSEAU
A coffee and the bill please... (following page)

This brief look at some of Paris's finest contemporary interiors makes it clear that the definition of "capital of the nineteenth century" does not go far enough. A real spirit of competition between restaurateurs has allowed a revival, not only of the food, but of the setting in which the culinary ceremony takes place. That is where this true capital of gastronomy excels, making lunch or dinner in Paris a celebration for all the senses.

Gourmet Guidebook

The restaurants we have chosen to include here are those where the setting matches the food in quality, and which best offer the possibility of discovering the culinary diversity of Paris. The selection is subjective, and far from exhaustive; it is simply a snapshot of a gastronomic landscape in a constant state of evolution.

HISTORIC SETTINGS

ALAIN DUCASSE
Hôtel Plaza Athénée
25, avenue Montaigne, 75008
Tel: 01 53 67 65 00
It was with this historic Belle Époque hotel that Alain Ducasse sparked the renaissance of great gastronomy in the grand hotels of Paris, as Auguste Escoffier had practiced it before him. The decor by Patrick Jouin has been improved by the addition of a magnificent contemporary chandelier with its cloud of pendant glass drops (see photo p. 35). But the best reason for coming here is the top-notch cuisine, expressed by one of the most highly skilled teams in the Parisian culinary scene and headed by Christophe Moret, formerly of Spoon.

LES AMBASSADEURS
Hôtel de Crillon
10, place de la Concorde, 75008
Tel: 01 44 71 16 16
ambassadeurs@crillon.com
www.crillon.com
Jean-François Piège, from the Ducasse stable, has earned two Michelin stars. A truly historic interior like that at the Hôtel de Crillon is a perfect match for him (see photos pp. 38–41).

LE BRISTOL
112, rue du Faubourg-Saint-Honoré, 75008
Tel: 01 53 43 43 00
resa@lebristolparis.com
Winter in the perfectly preserved Regency dining room, which was once the private theater of Jules de Castellane when this was a private residence; summer outside, in the immense private garden, which used to house a cloister. Eric Fréchon's cuisine is among the tastiest and most refined in the capital.

LE CINQ
George V
31, avenue George V, 75008
Tel: 01 49 52 71 54
cinq.par@fourseasons.com
www.fourseasons.com/paris/vacations/dining_77.html
Philippe Legendre and Éric Beaumard should need no introduction —although for the record they are, respectively, winners of Meilleur Ouvrier de France and Sommelier of the Year—and here they reign over one of the most elegant tables in Paris. The food and the service are both so naturally subtle that you could almost forget how magnificent they are. The restaurant was decorated, along with the rest of this luxury hotel, by Pierre-Yves Rochon, in a spirit that combines its 1900 past with more modern ideas of comfort.

LE GRAND VÉFOUR
17, rue de Beaujolais, 75001
Tel: 01 42 96 56 27
vefour@relaischateaux.com
www.relaischateaux.com/en/search-book/hotel-restaurant/vefour
Perhaps the most beautiful historic restaurant in Paris, with a decor that is difficult to date, but is somewhere between the Directoire and Restoration periods. Guy Martin's cuisine is up-to-the-minute, but still satisfies those who are nostalgic for the classics (see photos pp. 1, 20–27).

LA GRANDE CASCADE
Allée de Longchamp
Bois de Boulogne, 75016
Tel: 01 45 27 33 51
contact@lagrandecascade.fr
www.lagrandecascade.fr
Napoleon III's private pavilion at the heart of the Bois de Boulogne, enhanced during the 1900 Exposition Universelle by the addition of a superb glass canopy. A reasonable and regular venue appreciated by Parisians in need of fresh air.

LAPÉROUSE
51, quai des Grands-Augustins, 75006
Tel: 01 43 26 68 04
restaurantlaperouse@wanadoo.fr
Worth a visit for its private dining rooms and the unique Belle Époque atmosphere, even if the great Topolinski, the high priest of the Parisian night out, has never been replaced (see photos pp. 28–33).

LASSERRE
17, avenue Franklin-Roosevelt, 75008
Tel: 01 43 59 53 43
lasserre@lasserre.fr
www.restaurant-lasserre.com
With its opening roof and a typically 1950s atmosphere, which enchanted Salvador Dalí, Lasserre was both the first of the great contemporary designs and the ultimate manifestation of the classic French restaurant. Today it offers the quiet charm of old-fashioned service, in the hands of the famous manager Monsieur Louis, and the contemporary and sometimes audacious young talent of chef Jean-Louis Nomicos.

LAURENT
41, avenue Gabriel, 75008
Tel: 01 42 25 00 39
A pavilion built by Jacques-Ignace Hittorff in 1844 on the Champs-Élysées, this restaurant is one of the high altars of Parisian gastronomy. The chef Alain Perouget brilliantly interprets a menu devised by Joël Robuchon. Don't miss the fabulous *art pompier* paintings collected by the previous owner, the press tycoon Jimmy Goldsmith.

LUCAS CARTON
9, place de la Madeleine, 75008
Tel: 01 42 65 22 90
lucas.carton@lucascarton.com
www.lucascarton.com
The brilliantly simple Art Nouveau decor has just successfully come through a major facelift. Alain Senderens, in giving back his three stars to Michelin, has indicated that he wants to turn the page on classicism and open up to modernity (see photos pp. 46–51).

MAXIM'S
3, rue Royale, 75008
Tel: 01 42 65 27 94
www.maxims-de-paris.com
Pierre Cardin has turned Maxim's into an international brand name, but a visit to the place where it all started is worth it: nothing has really changed here since 1900 (except the public, perhaps, which is less and less Parisian). The classic example of the restaurant-museum (see photos pp. 42–45).

LA MÉDITERRANÉE
2, Place de l'Odéon, 75006
Tel: 01 43 26 02 30
www.la-mediterranee.com
Frescoes by Christian Bérard and Marcel Vertès, menus drawn by Cocteau, splendid terrace looking onto the Théâtre de l'Odéon. This fish restaurant opened in 1944, and perhaps with Denis Rippa from L'Ambroisie, it now has the chef it needs to become a Parisian great.

LE MEURICE
228, rue de Rivoli, 75001
Tel: 01 44 58 10 55
restauration@meuricehotel.com
www.meuricehotel.com
Yannick Alleno has turned this from a rather dozy place into one of the most dynamic restaurants in Paris. An exciting contrast between rigorous, inventive cuisine, and Louis XV decor, as recreated by artisans at the beginning of the twentieth century (see photos pp. 36–37).

LE PRÉ CATELAN
route de Suresnes, 75016
Tel: 01 44 14 41 14
www.lenotre.fr
Flagship of the Lenôtre catering group of boutiques, cafés, and restaurants. An eighteenth-century folly built in 1905 in the heart of the Bois de Boulogne. Beneath the gold and stucco, Frédéric Anton, one of the

masters of current gastronomy, offers precise and up-to-the-minute cuisine.

LE PROCOPE
13, rue de l'Ancienne-Comédie, 75006
Tel: 01 40 46 79 00
procope@blanc.net
www.procope.com/en
The oldest café-restaurant in Paris bears the marks of so many successive modifications that, apart from the facade, the only truly historic thing about this brasserie is its name (see photos pp. 16, 18–19).

PRUNIER
16, avenue Victor-Hugo, 75116
Tel: 01 44 17 35 85
prunier@maison-prunier.fr
www.prunier.com
A classic 1920s Art Deco monument, entirely dedicated to caviar and seafood. A true landmark, a "sleeping beauty," which is in the process of winning back its place as the restaurant for the Parisian smart set (see photos pp. 15, 54–55).

LE RELAIS PLAZA
Hôtel Plaza Athénée
21, avenue Montaigne, 75008
Tel: 01 53 67 64 00
reservation@plaza-athenee-paris.com
www.plaza-athenee-paris.com
Decor from the 1930s inspired by the ocean liner *Le Normandie*, and contemporary chic brasserie cuisine devised by Alain Ducasse (see photos p. 34).

TAILLEVENT
15, rue Lamennais, 75008
Tel: 01 44 95 15 01
mail@taillevent.com
www.taillevent.com
In the former residence of the Duc de Morny, the Vrinat family maintains the tradition of pageantry where the service and the cuisine (today the chef is Alain Solivérès) are combined in a concerto of refinement.

BRASSERIES

BALZAR
49, rue des Écoles, 75005
Tel: 01 43 54 16 67
www.brasseriebalzar.com/en
A meeting place for academics at the Collège de France and the Sorbonne since the end of the nineteenth century. Entirely renovated in 1931 by Marcellen Cazes, the proprietor of Lipp. The authentic spirit has been preserved, perhaps more than in any other brasserie, largely thanks to the solid conservatism and corporate solidarity of the regular customers.

AU BŒUF COURONNÉ
188, boulevard Jean-Jaurès, 75019
Tel: 01 42 39 44 44
au.boeuf.couronne@wanadoo.fr
www.rest-gj.com
Facing the old abattoirs at La Villette, this meeting point for wholesale butchers and livestock merchants has remained one of the best meat restaurants in the capital, and has kept its typically 1950s decor.

BOFINGER
5-7, rue de la Bastille, 75004
Tel: 01 42 72 87 82
www.bofingerparis.com/en
Authentic Art Deco interiors and Alsace brasserie cuisine unchanged for a century. Bofinger has maintained its tradition with a fresh public from the nearby Opéra Bastille (see photos pp. 58–63).

BOUILLON RACINE
3, rue Racine, 75003
Tel: 01 44 32 15 60
bouillon-racine@wanadoo.fr
www.bouillon-racine.com
Beveled mirrors, stained glass and opaline, carved wood paneling and marble mosaics, letters ornamented in gold leaf. Here, Art Nouveau expresses itself with baroque profusion. Restored in 1996 and listed as a historic monument, this former Chartier

bouillon still provides popular fare, bringing tourists and students together around the tables.

BRASSERIE LIPP
151, boulevard Saint-Germain, 75006
Tel: 01 45 48 72 93
www.brasserie-lipp.fr
A political and intellectual meeting place of long standing, which is still a stronghold of Saint-Germain-des-Prés nostalgia. The protocol is as unyielding as the court of Louis XIV (see photos pp. 57, 64–67).

LE CAFÉ DU COMMERCE
51, rue du Commerce, 75015
Tel: 01 45 75 03 27
www.lecafeducommerce.com
This former canteen for car workers, now run by Marie and Étienne Guerraud, was completely renovated in 1988. The only restaurant in Paris apart from Lasserre (see above) with a roof that opens. Notable for the quality of its meats, and fast becoming one of the hotspots of the fifteenth arrondissement.

CHARLOT-ROI DES COQUILLAGES
12, place Clichy, 75009
Tel: 01 53 20 48 00
de.charlot@blanc.net
www.charlot-paris.com
Furnishings from 1925, engraved glass partitions and seascape frescoes: the Art Deco at Charlot is exuberant and full of detail, hand in hand with the most extensive trays of seafood in Paris.

LA CLOSERIE DES LILAS
171, boulevard du Montparnasse, 75006
Tel: 01 40 51 34 50
Once a skating rink, then a dance hall, then a bar, and in becoming an American-style bar (and incidentally a restaurant) has set itself up as a meeting place for writers, whose names are carved on the tables they were supposed to occupy. For those curious to know what La Closerie looked like in

the nineteenth century, there is a very fine picture in one of the dining rooms at Laurent (see above).

LA COUPOLE
102, boulevard du Montparnasse, 75014
Tel: 01 43 20 14 20
cmonteiro@groupeflo.fr
www.flobrasseries.com/coupoleparis/en
The largest brasserie of the 1920s, still as vibrant and animated as ever, with its pillars decorated by the artists of the time, its grid of tables and seats, its bar, its terrace and even its dance floor, still in use today (see photos pp. 80–83).

FERMETTE MARBEUF 1900
5, rue Marbeuf, 75008
Tel: 01 53 23 08 00
fermettemarbeuf@blanc.net
www.fermettemarbeuf.com/en
An interior from 1900, rediscovered and patiently restored between 1978 and 1982, then listed as a historic monument in 1983. This glazed pavilion situated in the courtyard of a private house is the last specimen of a much-appreciated specialty of the end of the nineteenth century, the "winter garden" restaurant. This one was transformed into a brasserie by the Blanc brothers.

GALLOPIN
40, rue Notre-Dame-des-Victoires, 75002
Tel: 01 42 36 45 38
www.brasseriegallopin.com
The first English bar in Paris, with dark wood paneling and copper everywhere. Gallopin is still a popular meeting place in the business quarter of La Bourse (see photos pp. 68–71).

LE GRAND COLBERT
4, rue Vivienne, 75002
Tel: 01 42 86 87 88
le.grand.colbert@wanadoo.fr
This brasserie opposite the Galerie Colbert has a spectacular reconstruction of a mid-nineteenth-century interior, better than the real thing.

Gourmet Guidebook

(see photos pp. 106–109).

JULIEN
16, rue du Faubourg-Saint-Denis, 75010
Tel: 01 47 70 12 06
www.flobrasseries.com/brasseries
One of the most sumptuous Art Nouveau *bouillons*. Boasts a mahogany bar attributed to Louis Majorelle, and on the walls, four Louis Trezel inlay works on glass with stud and pearl relief, depicting Byzantine beauties, in beautifully rich stucco frames.

MOLLARD
115, rue Saint-Lazare, 75008
Tel: 01 43 87 50 22
espace.clients@mollard.fr
www.mollard.fr
A beautiful station brasserie with an eclectic decor of murals and paintings dated 1880, Mollard has won back its rank with a traditional menu and a great range of seafood (see photos pp. 72–75).

MONTPARNASSE 1900
59, boulevard du Montparnasse, 75006
Tel: 01 45 49 19 00
restaurant@montparnasse-1900.com
www.gerard-joulie.com/montparnasse_1900_3
A true *bouillon*, revamped in 1977 by Slavik who made it shine like new (perhaps a bit too much).

TERMINUS NORD
23, rue de Dunkerque, 75010
Tel: 01 42 85 05 15
www.terminusnord.com/en
This 1925 brasserie—as indicated by the sign above the outside menu—has kept its authenticity and its customer base of train lovers.

LE TRAIN BLEU
Place Louis-Arnaud, 75012
Tel: 01 43 43 09 06
isabelle.car@compass.group.fr
www.le-train-bleu.com
The most beautiful station buffet in the world. Le Train Bleu is to *art pompier* what the Sainte Chapelle is to Gothic architecture (see photos pp. 10–11 and 76–79).

VAGENENDE
142, boulevard Saint-Germain, 75006
Tel: 01 43 26 68 18
www.vagenende.fr
This carefully maintained and listed Art Nouveau Chartier *bouillon* has a classier atmosphere than those on the Right Bank, and really deserves a more inspired approach to the food.

LE ZÉPHYR
1, rue du Jourdain, 75020
Tel: 01 46 36 65 81
www.lezephyrcafe.com
Between Belleville and Buttes-Chaumont, the interior is pure Art Deco in this beautiful brasserie dated 1929. Such style is unexpected in this part of town. Traditional brasserie fare.

BISTROS

ALLARD
1, rue de l'Éperon, 75006
Tel: 01 43 26 48 23
A comfortable and upmarket bistro where diners enjoy copious amounts without a thought for cholesterol (see photos pp. 100–103).

L'AMI LOUIS
32, rue Vertbois, 75003
Tel: 01 48 87 77 48
The Americans' favorite Parisian bistro, with an interior unchanged since the 1930s (see photos pp. 104–105).

AU PETIT RICHE
25, rue Le Peletier, 75009
Tel: 01 47 70 68 68
aupetitriche@wanadoo.fr
www.aupetitriche.com/site.php
An opulent 1880 interior and traditional specialties from the Val de Loire (see photos pp. 86 and 88–89).

AUX LYONNAIS
32, rue Saint-Marc, 75002
Tel: 01 42 96 65 04
auxlyonnais@online.fr
www.alain-ducasse.com/public_us/cest_aussi/fr_aulyonnais
Typical 1900 decor with tiles that come straight from the Paris Metro.

Alain Ducasse has taken over the menu and turned it into a lovely Lyonnais-style table (see photos pp. 106–109).

LE BARATIN
3, rue Jouye-Rouve, 75020
Tel: 01 43 49 39 70
An unambitious interior, but Raquel Carena's cooking is definitely worth a visit (see photos pp. 85, 110–113).

BENOÎT
20, rue Saint-Martin, 75004
Tel: 01 42 72 45 68 / 01 42 72 25 76
This plush bistro has long been the haunt of councillors at the nearby Hôtel de Ville. Characterized by satirical posters from the 1930s and an ambience that has not changed since 1904. Recently taken over by Alain Ducasse, and in line for a reawakening.

BISTROT FLAUBERT
10, rue Gustave-Flaubert, 75017
Tel: 01 42 67 05 81
A lovely collection of Parisian slipware figures and old *Michelin Guides* adorns this annex to Michel Rostang's main restaurant. It offers accessibly priced, tasty food, notably delicious little stuffed vegetables in season.

BISTROT PAUL BERT
18, rue Paul-Bert, 75011
Tel: 01 43 72 24 01
A French version of the wine bar, where you keep a tab running for the evening, and what you eat is as important as what you drink. Over 300 wines are accompanied by solid offerings like velouté of lentils with foie gras, crunchy pig snout, or smoked andouillette cassoulet.

CHARDENOUX
1, rue Jules-Vallès, 75011
Tel: 01 43 71 49 52
An authentic workers' canteen, with a protected 1904 interior that has not changed a bit. The home cooking is very popular with the regulars.

CHARTIER
7, rue du Faubourg-Montmartre, 75009
Tel: 01 47 70 86 29
www.restaurant-chartier.com

The quintessential Parisian *bouillon* with simple, functional food and an interior to match (see photos pp. 94–95).

CHEZ MICHEL
10, rue de Belzunce, 75010
Tel: 01 44 53 06 20
Thierry Breton opened his bistro Chez Michel in 1995, just after Yves Camdeborde opened his, La Régalade (see below). The unpretentious decor dates back to 1939, but expect to be impressed: Breton did his apprenticeship at the Ritz, before working at top restaurants and hotels all over France. Sophisticated food based on authentic produce.

CHEZ PAUL
13, rue de Charonne, 75011
Tel: 01 47 00 34 57
The typical Parisian local bistro: checkered tablecloths, local customers, and your bill marked down on a slate as you go along.

LE CLOWN BAR
114, rue Amelot, 75011
Tel: 01 43 55 87 35
This wine bar is right next to the Cirque d'Hiver, and used to be part of the wings. Worth a visit for a frieze dated 1910 made by the tileworks at Sarreguemines representing a clown parade.

LE COMPTOIR
9, carrefour de l'Odéon, 75006
Tel: 01 44 27 07 97
Just around the corner from the Odéon, a new place for the founder of the Régalade (see below): a brasserie at lunchtime and an à la carte restaurant in the evening, from Monday to Friday. Yves Camdeborde sticks to the classics that made his reputation, like trotters off the bone or black pudding pâté.

L'ESCARGOT MONTORGUEIL
38, rue Montorgueil, 75001
Tel: 01 42 36 83 51
escargot-montorgueil@wanadoo.fr
www.escargot-montorgueil.com/index-gb.htm
A celebration of the snail since at least 1880. The stairs and shop front are original and the back room ceiling came from Sarah Bernhardt's private apartments (see photos pp. 90–93).

L'OS À MOELLE

3, rue Vasco de Gama, 75015
Tel: 01 45 57 27 27
Bistro food with a touch of haute cuisine: Thierry Faucher excels in the art of presentation and bringing the best out of simplicity. No actual decor as such, more of an ambience: that of a truly contemporary Parisian bistro. Good wine list.

LE POLIDOR

41, rue Monsieur-le-Prince, 75006
Tel: 01 43 26 95 34
lepolidor@aol.com
pageperso.aol.fr/lepolidor
An old dairy shop turned into a student restaurant at the heart of the Latin Quarter. Comparatively speaking, the prices are the same as they were in the 1920s (see photos pp. 96–99).

LA RÉGALADE

49, avenue Jean-Moulin, 75014
Tel: 01 45 45 68 58
This is where the bistro revolution started, in 1991. Yves Camdeborde bet on his native Béarn produce and brought a taste for simple and affordable food back to Paris. He has handed over to Bruno Doucet now, but the place is still a must, and it's still just as hard to get a table.

LE REPAIRE DE CARTOUCHE

8, boulevard des Filles-du-Calvaire or 99, rue Amelot, 75011
Tel: 01 47 00 25 86
The yellow wash and wood panels date from 1900. Modern bistro cuisine, delightfully served by Rodolphe Paquin from Normandy, one of four disciples expertly trained by Christian Constant at the Crillon.

LE SQUARE TROUSSEAU

1, rue Antoine-Vollon, 75012
Tel: 01 43 43 06 00
This 1900 popular restaurant has been partly restored and has kept its original spirit of a brasserie for local artisans (see photos pp. 2, 160).

LE VIEUX BISTROT

14, rue du Cloître Notre Dame, 75004
Tel: 01 43 54 18 95
On the Ile de la Cité, in the shadow of Notre Dame, an authentic old bistro maintains its traditional home-cooking

menu with the steady composure of Inspector Maigret. One can easily imagine him, sitting on one of the red benches, wolfing down the bœuf bourguignon.

CONTEMPORARY SETTINGS

RESTAURANT 1728

8, rue d'Anjou, 75008
Tel: 01 40 17 04 77
restaurant1728@wanadoo.fr
It is not so much the decor of this restaurant (which occupies the restored salons of the Hôtel d'Anjou where Lafayette lived) that is interesting, nor even the fusion cuisine, but the concept of a restaurant-gallery where all the artworks on the walls, both ancient and modern, are for sale.

L'ALCAZAR

62, rue Mazarine, 75006
Tel: 01 53 10 19 99
www.alcazar.fr/siteft_us
It's Conran down to the smallest details, a trendy brasserie where the food is carefully prepared, the atmosphere young but not exclusively so, and the bill steep but not outrageous (see photos pp. 13 and 144–147).

L'AMBROISIE

9, place des Vosges, 75004
Tel: 01 42 78 51 45
In a setting that reproduces a private house of the seventeenth century, splendidly recreated by François-Joseph Graf, a meal at L'Ambroisie is one of the great gastronomic experiences Paris has to offer. As its name suggests, it is the food of the gods (photos pp. 128–131).

L'APICIUS

20, rue d'Artois, 75008
Tel: 01 43 80 19 66
Don't be overwhelmed by the grand nineteenth-century building off the Champs-Élysées, or its princely garden owned by the filmmaker Luc Besson. Jean-Pierre Vigato has changed none of his culinary practices and still makes the best calf's head in Paris. Regulars from his "bistro" on avenue de Villiers

have followed him here: such unassuming talent, and such sublime dishes, are not easy to find in the west of Paris.

L'ARPÈGE

84, rue de Varenne, 75007
Tel: 01 47 05 09 06
arpege@alain-passard.com
www.alain-passard.com
The very sober decoration—Arman sculpture, Lalique glass, and a portrait of Alain Passard's grandmother on the wall—allows the culinary creations to stand out. Passard is one of the most original chefs in Paris. He has imposed an almost minimalist gastronomy by rediscovering vegetables and putting them at the center of his menus. But he is also a master at cooking meats to perfection; his dishes have something almost musical about them, both enigmatic and obvious.

L'ASTRANCE

4, rue Beethoven, 75016
Tel: 01 40 50 84 40
Five years at L'Arpège (see above) set free Pascal Barbot's taste for invention and creativity. This young chef—he's barely thirty—is the d'Artagnan of the new band of Parisian cooks. Audacity, flair, and generosity counterbalance a very juvenile provocative streak. His restaurant, with its modern but discreet decor, has become a hot spot of Parisian gastronomy.

L'ATELIER DE JOËL ROBUCHON

Hôtel Pont-Royal
5, rue Montalembert, 75007
Tel: 01 42 22 56 56
L'Atelier de Joël Robuchon caused quite a stir when it opened. It aimed for a new way of thinking about the restaurant, by opening up the kitchen onto the client space and putting that client space around a bar, which is supposed to encourage a friendly and communicative atmosphere. Very coherent design by Pierre-Yves Rochon, very precise food by Robuchon, but the whole set-up lacks a little warmth (see photos pp. 132–135).

L'ATELIER MAÎTRE ALBERT

1, rue Maître Albert, 75005
Tel: 01 56 81 30 01
ateliermaitrealbert@guysavoy.com

www.ateliermaitrealbert.com
A menu reworked by Guy Savoy, and an elegant and calm interior by Jean-Michel Wilmotte, at this truly contemporary rotisserie: "how Paris reinvented the inn at the turn of the twenty-first century."

LE BARFLY

49-51, avenue George V, 75008
Tel: 01 53 67 84 60
Miguel Cancio Martins seems to be the official decorator for the Paris nightlife, but also for that of London, Marbella, and Singapore. Buddha Bar in Paris, Man Ray in Paris, Los Angeles, and New York, Opium in London, Raffles in Singapore, Doc Cheng's in Hamburg: they're all his. Martins' eclecticism knows no bounds but at the same time he has a clearly recognizable touch. Barfly is an oversized lounge, an imagined American bar seen through the wrong end of a giant kaleidoscope. New York as only Paris dreams it.

BARLOTTI

35, place du Marché-Saint-Honoré, 75001
Tel: 01 44 86 97 97
barlotti@barlotti.fr
The look of this restaurant-lounge is inspired by the film *Blade Runner*. After Buddha Bar (see below), Barfly (see above), and Barrio Latino, this Italianesque venture is the fourth feather in the cap of the new prince of the trendy restaurant scene, Raymond Visan, from the group George V Restauration. Come here not just to get something to eat, but to experience that synthesis of food and all-out attention to atmosphere that Paris has started to call "le fooding."

BAROCCO

23, rue Mazarine, 75006
Tel: 01 43 26 40 24
Maurice Savinel and Roland Le Bévillon, the designers of the Byblos Hotel in Saint-Tropez, have created an inevitably warm environment for this Brazilian restaurant-bar-lounge where Parisian showbiz people love to congregate.

LE BÉLIER

13, rue des Beaux-Arts, 75006
Tel: 01 44 41 99 01

Gourmet Guidebook

Another superb apartment conceived by Jacques Garcia in his inimitable and distinctive style, which mixes First and Second Empire, Belle Époque, and baroque designs (see photos pp. 124–127).

BON
25, rue de la Pompe, 75016
Tel: 01 40 72 70 00
Satin-lined walls, candles, a fireplace, and a lovers' dining room: chef Bruno Brangea, former sous-chef at Flora Danica (see under La Maison du Danemark, below), has his work cut out to make us forget Philippe Starck's omnipresent baroque interior (see photos pp. 4–5, 120–121).

BON 2
2, rue du Quatre-Septembre, 75002
Tel: 01 44 55 51 55
Sofas in burnished leather, crystal chandeliers, Venetian mirrors, and a stainless-steel bar carrying the rates at the stock exchange. Bon 2 is a modern version of the brasserie Gallopin (see above).

BUDDHA BAR
8, rue Boissy D'Anglas, 75008
Tel: 01 53 05 90 00
More staggeringly kitsch than a Hollywood spectacular, this place is only incidentally about food. The design is a real eyeful, and the music an earful of remixes of remixes of remixes...

LE CABARET
2, place du Palais-Royal, 75001
Tel: 01 58 62 56 25
With Franco-fusion food, and an interior by Jacques Garcia and Ora Ito, this very trendy club is obviously still looking for its identity. Or perhaps it is happy to float aimlessly on the waves of fashion for a while longer.

CAFÉ BEAUBOURG
100, rue Saint-Martin, 75004
Tel: 01 48 87 63 96
Less interesting for the basic contemporary brasserie food than for Christian de Portzamparc's design. Severe but coherent, promoting aesthetic polished concrete, and featuring a spectacular staircase up to the mezzanine (see photo pp. 118).

CAFÉ DE L'ESPLANADE
52, rue Fabert, 75007
Tel: 01 47 05 38 80
Another manifestation of the Costes family, facing Les Invalides.

LE CAFÉ MARLY
Le Louvre, Cour Napoléon
93, rue de Rivoli, 75001
Tel: 01 49 26 06 60
Olivier Gagnère has successfully brought a touch of class to this space within the Louvre by furnishing it and dressing its walls with a discreet theatricality, avoiding showiness and incongruous effects (see photos pp. 8, 148–151).

LE CARRÉ DES FEUILLANTS
14, rue de Castiglione, 75001
Tel: 01 42 86 82 82
In a restaurant where the design extols the beauty of raw materials and raw art, Alain Dutournier brings together the gastronomic traditions of the southwestern Landes, the technique of haute cuisine, and an acute sense of innovation, to offer food which is both original and solidly anchored in regional produce, both refined and authentic (see photo p. 116).

LE CHIBERTA
3, rue Arsène Houssaye, 75008
Tel: 01 53 53 42 00
info@lechiberta.com
www.lechiberta.com
Now in the capable hands of Guy Savoy, with an interior designed by Jean-Michel Wilmotte and based around wine. A fun place where you can make an accessible journey in the culinary world of this great chef (see photos pp. 140–143).

CRISTAL ROOM DE BACCARAT
11, place des États-Unis, 75116
Tel: 01 40 22 11 10
www.baccarat.fr
Philippe Starck let himself go as never before at the Baccarat Cristal Room: chandeliers, seats, bare walls, and marble pillars, all slightly reminiscent of a Dalí painting (see photos pp. 152–153).

EMPORIO ARMANI CAFFE
149, boulevard Saint-Germain, 75006
Tel: 01 45 48 62 15

Designed by Armani and situated at the heart of the Armani store in Saint-Germain-des-Prés. The Italian cuisine based on seasonal produce is really very good, the service is masterfully managed by the charming and diligent Massimo Mori, and you can eat there quickly at any time. A must for fashion victims.

GEORGES
Centre Georges Pompidou
19, rue Beaubourg, 75004
Tel: 01 44 78 47 99
A very space-age design by a team of young avant-garde plastic artists. Georges has one of the prettiest views of Paris from the top of the Pompidou Center, and serves fusion food that is constantly improving (see photos pp. 115, 154–159).

LA GRANDE ARMÉE
3, avenue de la Grande-Armée, 75116
Tel: 01 45 00 24 77
One of the oldest addresses of the Costes group.

GUY SAVOY
18, rue Troyon, 75017
Tel: 01 43 80 40 61
www.guysavoy.com
Guy Savoy has had a leading place in the Parisian restaurant scene for several years now. His gastronomy is both sophisticated and native, profoundly rooted as it is in the *terroirs*, assuring him a longstanding international reputation even before being awarded a third Michelin star. For many visiting from abroad, his restaurant is the first port of call, after which they can say that they have at last arrived in France. The design by Jean-Michel Wilmotte features primitive African and Asian statues and paintings by the Cobra group, reflecting Savoy's exacting and lyrical cuisine (see photo p. 119).

HÔTEL COSTES
239, rue Saint-Honoré, 75001
Tel: 01 42 44 50 25
www.hotelcostes.com
A fine Napoleonic maze designed by Jacques Garcia, and one of his indisputable successes.

IL PALAZZO
Normandy Hôtel
7, rue de l'Échelle, 75001
Tel: 01 42 60 91 20
Designer Marc Dumas has brought a touch of modernity to this establishment, with bronze bells hung above the rows of tables and neo-baroque furnishing. The frescoes on the ceiling and fireplace in this hotel restaurant, however, have not changed since 1877. The food is Italian, *à la française.*

LE JARDIN
Hôtel Royal Monceau
37, avenue Hoche, 75008
Tel: 01 42 99 98 70
The rotunda of the Royal Monceau hotel has been transformed into a Napoleonic tent. Drapes, Second Empire chairs, bundles of lances are clearly the work of Jacques Garcia, whose work has become synonymous internationally with the renovation of luxury hotels. The food is nicely Provençal.

LE JULES VERNE
Tour Eiffel, Champ-de-Mars, 75007
Tel: 01 45 55 61 44
Slavik's last masterpiece, where he tempered his baroque tendencies and fused nicely with the cast-iron world of Gustave Eiffel (see photos pp. 122–123).

MAISON BLANCHE
Théâtre des Champs-Élysées
15, avenue Montaigne, 75008
Tel: 01 47 23 55 99
www.maison-blanche.fr
Jacques and Laurent Pourcel, the twin brothers from Montpellier, have their Paris annex on the terrace of the Théâtre des Champs-Élysées. The building, by the great architect Auguste Perret, dates from 1913 and is an architectural tour de force in its own right. The modern structure stands clear of the historic monument by means of independent posts, supported like a suspension bridge. The space has been decorated by Imaad Rahmouni, an acolyte of Philippe Starck. The Window Room gives a dizzying vertical feel, its single glass wall overhanging the west of Paris. The Mezzanine on the upper level opens

onto wider views of the landscape and reveals surprises like a phosphorescent bar with changing colors, and a further terrace, an islet of greenery within the city. The food is "Languedoc revisited," strong in contrasts, or flirting with similarities, but always on a playful and slightly experimental note.

LA MAISON DU DANEMARK
142, avenue des Champs-Élysées, 75008
Tel: 01 44 13 86 26
www.restaurantfloradanica.com
The two restaurants of the Danish cultural center, the Flora Danica and the Copenhague, were refurbished in 2002, but still have a very 1970s look about them. This is where you can find *saumon à l'unilatérale*, the "salmon for purists" that won Paris over when it appeared on the menu of the Copenhague in 1974.

MARKET
15, avenue Matignon, 75008
Tel: 01 56 43 40 90
prmarketsa@aol.com
The partnership of two stars: Vongerichten (Jean-Georges to his friends) devising the food and Christian Liaigre designing the interior, both names in their own right in New York. Jean-Georges is fast becoming the most high-profile French restaurateur in the United States with his (slightly) fusion approach, and Liaigre has remodeled the Mercer Hotel in New York's Soho. Here he has chosen to create a warm room where primitive art statues in stone, wood, and glass stare each other down. The menu includes tuna and wasabi, lobster and radish, and satay chicken, which do not easily convince Parisian palates.

MICHEL ROSTANG
20, rue Rennequin, 75017
Tel: 01 47 63 40 77
rostang@relaischateaux.com
www.michelrostang.com
Michel Rostang is at home in his restaurant with a cozy English club feel, delighting diners with what he does best: solid but refined *cuisine bourgeoise* such as veal shank, fattened Bresse chicken, whole veal sweetbread. The produce is not dressed up or disguised, just brought

to its point of perfection by precise cooking and a strict art of preparation.

LE MURAT
1, boulevard Murat, 75016
Tel: 01 46 51 33 17
One of Jacques Garcia's most successful interiors, on the theme of the Grande Armée of the Napoleonic Wars: grenadiers' shakos, blood-red chairs, and sofas ornamented with a leopard-skin stripe, violet and almond-green silk curtains hiding one or two alcoves, and the walls and ceiling covered with silver birch trunks. Wow.

PERSHING HALL
49, rue Pierre Charron, 75008
Tel: 01 58 36 58 36
www.pershing-hall.com
A very "designed" place, with large, pink transparent panels, vases and chairs in stern red, and a patio overhung by an impressive vertical garden. It is impossible to remain indifferent to Andrée Putman's design. The cuisine wears its fusion tendencies on its sleeve. Modernity on display, for all to see and eat.

PINXO
9, rue d'Alger, 75001
Tel: 01 40 20 72 00
A modern but unaggressive setting, which encourages a convivial atmosphere. Pinxo is a paradigm for the bistro of tomorrow (see photos pp. 136–139).

RESTAURANT PIERRE GAGNAIRE
6, rue Balzac, 75008
Tel: 01 58 36 12 50
www.pierre-gagnaire.com/anglais
Pierre Gagnaire is carrying out one of the most unusual experiments in the history of French cooking. With the help of the chemist Hervé This, he has perfected a "molecular gastronomy" that seeks the true nature of ingredients at the level of the chemical processes at work in different types of cooking. This provides a natural impetus to creativity, not just for making new dishes but also for finding completely new ways of cooking: chantilly butter, chantilly cheese, warm aspic, or flank steak in soup. The decor of his restaurant is sober to the point of austerity.

SPOON, WINE AND FOOD
14, rue de Marignan, 75008
Tel: 01 40 76 34 44
If there had to be just one "fusion" restaurant in the world, this would be it, set up by Alain Ducasse at the beginning of the new millennium. Rather than an assortment of flavors, this is cuisine built on the mastery of the most diverse techniques: modern ones, like induction, steam, and vacuum; exotic ones like plancha and wok; and traditional ones like pressure-cooking, grilling, and rotisserie. All for the benefit of a completely flexible meal, where everybody, from Asia to America and from France to Africa, can compose their own gastronomic itinerary without risking getting it wrong. A bare but elegant light-grey decor gives the place a refreshing serenity.

LA TABLE DE JOËL ROBUCHON
16, avenue Bugeaud, 75016
Tel: 01 56 28 16 16
A very experienced team now presides over the destiny of what was once the Seize au Seize. The young Frédéric Simonin, former right-hand man to Ghislaine Arabian, is proving to be an outstanding chef. A string of creations using ingredients in small portions allows guests to appreciate the extent of his talent. Antoine Hernandez is the seasoned, friendly manager and François Benot is one of the most promising pastry chefs in Paris. Joël Robuchon, at the top, is standing by his intention to place great food within the reach of (almost) every budget. The caramel-colored decor is chic and functional without being too intrusive, making the whole experience a restful one.

TERRASSE MIRABEAU
5, place de Barcelone, 75016
Tel: 01 42 24 41 51
Pierre Negrevergne, previously with Michel Rostang (see above), is just as capable of dashing off dishes in the bistro style as devising more sophisticated preparations. His simple, modern-looking neo-bistro is one of the better addresses in this well-to-do neighborhood.

TOKYO EAT
Palais de Tokyo
13, avenue du Président Wilson, 75016
Tel: 01 47 20 00 29
The space alone is worth a visit. The room within the Palais de Tokyo, shared with the City of Paris Museum of Modern Art, looks more like an aircraft hangar than a restaurant. Chef Thierry Bassard and manager Claudio Episcopo have festooned it with large pink flying saucers that honk out brisk techno music. Something is out there... and it's the fusion food, which is *way* out there. Welcome to the hyper-trendy world of "fooding." Despite this, the prices are reasonable, the service comes with a smile, and the customers are a mix. Not surprisingly, it's doing fantastically well.

ZE KITCHEN GALERIE
4, rue des Grands-Augustins, 75006
Tel: 01 44 32 00 32
William Ledeuil, who used to work with Guy Savoy at Les Bouquinistes, opened this handsome space in 2001. The decor is postmodern and the place is just a little too noisy. The menu is entirely dedicated to fusion—Guy Savoy being one of the Parisian masters. As a devotee of Thai cooking, he has developed a technique for using Asian roots and herbs in the French culinary tradition. His authentic source for ingredients is Paris's Chinatown in the thirteenth arrondissement, but he visits the floating market in Bangkok several times a year, and imports from as far away as Japan.

Pierre Rival would like to thank his gourmet muses, Aliona Antonova, Stéphanie Lux, Olga Moroz, Emmanuelle Perrier, Catherine Sick, and Sophie Tao, and his tasting companions, Serge Cosseron, Jacques Dereux, Albert Nahmias, Alain Neyman, Jean-Claude Ribaut, Anton Rival, and Christian Sarramon. He also thanks Ghislaine Bavoillot for being both so demanding and so generous with the freedom she has granted him, as well as the whole team at Flammarion for their unbending perseverance.

Christian Sarramon would like to thank Inès, Diego, and Kim who are not averse to a good meal. Thanks to Pierre Rival for having exhumed the history of each place so well. Thank you also to Gisou Bavoillot, Sylvie Ramaut, and Aurélie Sallandrouze for their constant assistance.

Editorial Director Ghislaine Bavoillot
Translated from the French by Joseph West
Copyediting Lindsay Porter
Art Director and Graphic Design Isabelle Ducat
Typesetting Thierry Renard
Proofreading Penelope Isaac
Color Separation Reproscan

Distributed in North America by Rizzoli International Publications, Inc.

Originally published in French as
Paris gourmet : belles et bonnes tables de la ville
© Éditions Flammarion, 2005
English-language edition
© Éditions Flammarion, 2006

www.editions.flammarion.com

06 07 08 4 3 2 1

FC0508-06-III
ISBN-10: 2-0803-0508-5
ISBN-13: 9782080305084
Dépôt légal: 03/2006

Printed in Italy by Errestampa